THE JAPANESE
ELECTION SYSTEM

The Japanese Diet was set up under the strong influence of the allied forces. The resultant one-party rule by the Liberal Democratic Party was widely criticized until the party system was modified in 1993. There followed an unprecedented change in the Diet, representing the first multi-member districts with single nontransferable voting and the consequent unequal apportionment were replaced by proportional representation and single-member districts with plurality.

In *The Japanese Election System* these systems are examined using models of game theory and rational choice. Features of Japanese politics today, such as factional politics and one-party democratic rule, are the direct result of recognition of the failings in its old system. However, using game theory and models of rational choice, the author demonstrates that the old election system had benefits which do not exist in the current system and concludes that there is still a need for change.

This is a unique analysis of the present Japanese political system which will interest both political economists and non-specialists alike. For the first time approaches used to analyse American and European political systems are applied to 'mysterious' Japan.

Junichiro Wada received his Bachelor's and Master's degrees from Hitotsubashi University and his Ph.D. from the University of Maryland. He is now an Associate Professor at Yokohama City University. His major field of interest is public economics, especially public choice, and his articles have been published in many leading Japanese journals.

ROUTLEDGE STUDIES IN THE GROWTH ECONOMIES OF ASIA

THE JAPANESE ELECTION SYSTEM

Three analytical perspectives

Junichiro Wada

London and New York

First published 1996
by Routledge
11 New Fetter Lane, London EC4P 4EE

Simultaneously published in the USA and Canada
by Routledge
29 West 35th Street, New York, NY 10001

Reprinted 1997

Typeset in Garamond by LaserScript, Mitcham, Surrey
Printed in Great Britain by
T.J. International, Padstow, Cornwall

British Library Cataloguing in Publication Data
A catalogue record for this book is available from the British Library

Library of Congress Cataloguing in Publication Data
Wada, Junichiro, 1960–
the Japanese election System: three analytical perspectives
/ Junichiro Wada.
p. cm. – (Routledge studies in the growth economies of Asia.
ISSN 1359–7876 : 5)
Includes bibliographical references.
1. Elections – Japan. 2. Representative government and representation
– Japan. 3. Political parties – Japan. 4. Japan – Politics and
Government – 1989– I. Title. II. Series.
JQ1692.W33 1996
324.6'3'0952"dc20   95-20530

ISBN 0–415–14009–9
ISSN 1359–7876

For Fumie

CONTENTS

ACKNOWLEDGEMENTS

The purpose of this book is to demonstrate that non-Japanese and non-experts in political science can understand many features of the Japanese election system. To understand means not only to gain knowledge but also to explain Japanese politics by using the same approach as that used by non-Japanese formal theorists of political science or economists to explain their country's politics. I hope this book will thank the Rotary Club, which sent me to the University of Maryland for better international understanding, and the University of Maryland, which gave me a graduate assistantship and allowed me to devote my time to my studies.

To achieve the objective of this book, the help of non-Japanese who know the theory and the facts very well was indispensable. If the book succeeds in attracting the interest of non-Japanese scholars, it will in large part be due to the contribution of my academic adviser, Mancur Olson. Since the book is my Ph.D. dissertation for the University of Maryland, I have been greatly influenced by its faculty members. Chapter 1 was written upon the strong recommendation of Dennis Mueller. The ideas in Chapter 2 appeared when I was attending Peter Coughlin's lecture and it was presented at the Public Economics workshop organized by Martin McGuire. Chapter 3 was originally a term paper for H. Peyton Young's class, and David Lalman encouraged me on to its completion. Chapter 4 was a contribution to Andrew Lyon's seminar. I really appreciate the help of Wallace Oates and Robert Schwab, who continued to give me comments until the final stage. I studied game theory outside the department, and so I must thank John Horowitz, Joe Oppenheimer, Joseph Harrington and the outreach program of George Mason University for their input.

Since the theme of the book is the Japanese election system,

ACKNOWLEDGEMENTS

study in Japan was also critical. I am grateful for the help of Hiromitsu Ishi, who has taught me since my undergraduate days. Chapter 4 was inspired by his empirical work. At Hitotsubashi University I also received advice from Yukio Noguchi, Kotaro Suzumura, Eiji Tajika and Koichi Tadenuma. I also acknowledge the comments of my classmate, Midori Hirokawa. After returning to Japan I completed this book while I presented the ideas in some seminars. Chapters 1, 2 and 3 were reported at the Institute of Statistical Studies. I appreciate the comments of Yasushi Iino, Masahiro Fukaya, Naoyuki Yoshino, Toshihiro Ihori and Koichi Takita. Chapter 2 was also reported at the Japan Institute of Public Finance and the Japan Association of Economics and Econometrics. I wish to thank Taro Ozawa and Tetsuya Kishimoto for their helpful comments. Chapter 3 was also reported at the Japanese Public Choice Society at Keio University, which is supported by Hiroshi Kato, and the Game Theory Seminar at the University of Tokyo. I thank those present for their comments. Fukashi Horie and Yoshiaki Kobayashi seconded me for membership of the Japan Election Studies Association and I studied much there. I must also express my gratitude to Steven Reed and Gary Cox, who sent me some comments by letters.

Since the book is written in English and its object is to help non-Japanese people to understand Japanese politics, editing by native English-speakers was crucial. I am grateful to my classmates, Lawrence Yun, Jonathan Dunn, John Guyton and my colleague, Marianne Santillo.

My academic adviser, Mancur Olson, continued to urge me to write a dissertation that could be understood by non-experts and strongly recommended me to ask non-experts to read it. This job was done by my wife, Fumie. Though she skipped all the maths equations, which she is allergic to, she understood all that I wanted to say in the book. I dedicate it to her as representing non-expert readers in this area.

1

INTRODUCTION

Explaining Japanese political economy without invoking the argument of a "Japanese special character"

The rule of the Liberal Democratic Party (L.D.P.) ended in 1993. After a money scandal involving former L.D.P. vice-governor (deputy party leader) Shin Kanemaru, one L.D.P. faction, led by former L.D.P. secretary general Ichiro Ozawa, left the party and created a new one called "Shinsei-to" (the Japan Renewal Party, or J.R.P.). In the Lower House election following this, the L.D.P. could not get a majority without the Ozawa faction. The Ozawa faction formed a coalition government with all the anti-L.D.P. parties except the Japan Communist Party (J.C.P.). The Ozawa faction had been "owned" at first by former prime minister Kakuei Tanaka and later by former prime minister Noboru Takeshita. Both of them resigned because of bribery scandals. Actually, Shin Kanemaru also belonged to this faction. At one time it was the biggest faction in the L.D.P. and was considered to be able to obtain and use the most money. If one thinks of anti-L.D.P. parties as uncorrupt and unconcerned about having seats in the cabinet, it might seem strange that the critics of the L.D.P.'s "money politics" or corruption formed a coalition government with this faction.

In order to avoid public criticism of money politics, Japanese politicians changed the election rules. Their logic is as follows.

For electoral purposes Japan is divided into 129 districts which elect 511 representatives. Each district chooses two to six representatives by single non-transferable voting (S.N.T.V.). Under this rule voters can choose only one name, though the districts elect more than one representative. The combination of multi-member districts with S.N.T.V. forces L.D.P. politicians to compete against each other in the same district. Since they must espouse the same party's policy,[1] ideological differences become irrelevant and they are led into pork-barrel politics. Moreover, in the election they argue that they need money to compete with each other. (See, for example, Ozawa 1993.) This typical politicians' logic to explain Japanese money politics is not their own invention. Many journalists and political scientists, including Ishikawa (1981, 1984, 1990), Sakagami (1990), and Iwai (1991) have also accepted this logic.

Voting by multi-member districts with S.N.T.V. has been the most notable characteristic of Japanese elections. Some people seek a two-party system like that in the United Kingdom or the United States and support the single-member plurality system. Others advocate a proportional representation system to keep some proportionality between popular support and party strength.

Finally, at the beginning of 1994, the Diet dared to create a new electoral system by dividing the number of the members of the Lower House in two and using both systems together. They did this without foresight. They passed a new law providing that 300 Lower House members would be chosen by a single-member district plurality system and 200 would be chosen separately by a proportional representation system with a party-decided list of candidates. For the election of the 200 the country is divided into eleven areas.[2] The next election will be held under this new rule.

This outcome is the result of a simple compromise between the L.D.P. and the Ozawa group, who support a single-member district plurality system, and anti-L.D.P. parties, which support a proportional representation system. On television shows, in magazines, and in newspapers many political scientists support this compromise, but not on the basis of any serious research. We should seriously study the new and the old election systems.

Are multi-member districts so bad? Pork-barrel polities can exist in either single-member plurality systems or proportional systems. Multi-member districts may be better if they reduce over-specialized pork-barrels in single-member districts or strong pressure from nationwide groups in a proportional representation system, either of which causes a big political distortion in the economy. We definitely need serious study of this issue. We need more theoretical evaluation of the new and the old Japanese election systems.

As the Japanese economy grows, Japan's politics, and especially the politics of the ruling party for almost forty years, the L.D.P., attract the interest of many scholars. "The L.D.P.'s factional politics" and "a stable L.D.P. government" are often talked about. Many researchers attribute these characteristics to the special character of the Japanese people.

"The L.D.P.'s factional politics" are often considered by American scholars like Thayer (1969), Baerwald (1986) or Curtis (1988) and by some Japanese scholars, including Kodaira (1985), to be the product of the Japanese cultural tradition of bossism.[3] They say that the reason for the "stable L.D.P. government," which continued for more than forty years,[4] is mainly the good condition of the Japanese economy and that condition, in turn, tends to be explained by Japanese culture or philosophy.

There is circularity in this logic. "The characteristics of Japanese politics derive from the characteristics of Japanese." We cannot get any useful insight from such a statement. Many topics should probably be explained by "rules" or "institutional constraints" that Japan has adopted, not by the special character of the Japanese people or society. An analysis and evaluation of Japanese political economy using the same basic assumptions as are used to analyze European or U.S. political economy should be attempted.

The election of multi-member districts with single non-transferable voting and unequal apportionment

Compared with the United States, Japan uses many different political institutions or "rules", including unitary (non-federal) government, the prime minister system, and a strictly selected meritocratic bureaucracy, to name but a few. However, in this book I will focus on themes related to the most controversial issue, the electoral rules. The Japanese system appears to be clearly different from the European or U.S. systems. The electoral rules explain some important features of Japanese political economy, including "the L.D.P.'s factional politics" and "the stable L.D.P. government."

The two most distinguishing characteristics of the old Japanese election system were multi-member districts with single non-transferable voting and unequal apportionment. As indicated earlier, the election of multi-member districts with S.N.T.V. has been the most notable characteristic of Japanese elections and has often been considered a "bad" system.

The apportionment of representatives in Japan is unfair by any

3

standard. Small population prefectures have more representatives than bigger population prefectures, as we can see in Table 23. It has been shown that this causes a political distortion in the Japanese budget (Ishi *et al.* 1981a, b, 1983, Fujimoto 1983, Ogura 1984, Wada 1985, etc.). For example, Wada (1985) showed that each prefecture's administrative investment from the national budget can be explained mainly by the number of politicians, not by egalitarian considerations.

The current election reforms may correct this unfair representation system a little, but not completely. (See Table 24.) The Lower House slipped in a rule that is advantageous for less populous prefectures. It provided one seat for each prefecture at first, and after that the rest of the seats are assigned by the method of largest remainders.[5] Because of this rule, if we add the single-member district parts to proportional representation parts, the Minami-Kanto proportional representation area (Chiba, Kanagawa and Yamanashi) has fewer representatives than the Tokai area (Gifu, Shizuoka, Aichi and Mie), although its population is higher.[6]

It is useful to start with the origins of the characteristics of the Japanese election system.

A history of Japanese election system from the viewpoint of election theory

The modern history of Japan since the opening up of the country in 1854 (with the Kanagawa Treaty) or the Meiji Restoration in 1868 is usually discussed as two eras, before and after World War II. Since multi-member districts with single non-transferable voting (S.N.T.V.) appeared before World War II and unequal apportionment appeared after the war, we will separate the history of Japanese election system into those two eras.

The electoral system before World War II: introducing single non-transferable voting

Multi-member districts with S.N.T.V. are sometimes called "elections Japanese style." This label may be suitable. S.N.T.V. is used in every level of elections in Japan but is hardly ever used in other countries. However, it would be wrong to imagine this rule has been used from the beginning of modern Japanese politics. It was advocated by a bureaucrat, Kametaro Hayashida, around 1893 and

4

adopted at the prefectural level in 1899 and at the national level in 1900.[7] Let us look back at the earlier history of the Japanese electoral system.

Japan started to move toward full-scale parliamentary politics after the opening of the country in 1854. The idea of parliamentary politics can be seen in the "Gokajo no Goseimon" (Imperial Oath) of the Meiji Restoration in 1868. But in its early stages the Meiji government was an autocratic government of "Hambatsu" (feudal cliques) and aristocrats. The Jiyu Minken Undo (the Freedom and People's Rights Movement), which agitated for a parliament, was oppressed by the Shukai Jorei (the Public Assembly Ordinance) and other severe restrictions. After the government scandal of 1881,[8] the Emperor, in effect the government, finally promised to establish a parliament within ten years. The Hambatsu and aristocrats, who had become the bureaucrats, reluctantly agreed to create a parliament and a constitution.

The electoral law governing the Lower House was promulgated with the Meiji Imperial Constitution in 1889.[9] Even though there had been many debates about the electoral system in the government,[10] it finally became very similar to British electoral law at that time, which had both single-member and two-member constituencies. Two hundred and fourteen single-member districts for every 130,000 people were designated. Forty-three two-member districts were created where a county had to be divided to conform to this population size. Since the lawmakers thought suffrage should be given to "eminent" persons "who represent the people in each district", the representatives were assigned in proportion to the population and not in proportion to the number of voters.[11] We should notice that they used multi-voting for two-member districts without any prominent dispute. Multi-voting means that each voter has as many votes as there are seats in the district. Since they used a non-cumulative type, voters wrote down two different names in two-member districts. This rule may seem natural to Americans, but typical contemporary Japanese might imagine that in the Meiji era people used the single voting rule. Japanese now enter just one name in any multi-member district. In fact, single non-transferable voting for multi-member districts is now universal in Japan, from the election of an elementary school's committee to the National Diet.

Multi-voting was not only the straight introduction of a European or American system but also a natural rule for Japanese

5

people at the time. From Haruhara (1962a, b, 1963) or the Ide family document (1629–1874) we can see that during the Edo (Tokugawa) era (1603–1868) village or town autonomies used multi-voting for their elections. After the Meiji Restoration, prefectural governors were appointed by the Meiji central government, and some of them had local assemblies. Multi-voting was used for the Minkai (a prefectural assembly before 1878 which was not authorized by the central government), the Fukenkai (the prefectural assembly which was established by law in 1878), and the Shichosonkai (the local assembly which was established by law in 1888). We must note that the laws on the elections for such assemblies do not say anything about multi-voting. It may have been the common sense thing for the multi-member district elections at that time in Japan. We can see for a fact that they used multi-voting in elections to the Minkai and the Fukenkai and in the provision of the law that, if there were more names on the ballot paper, one had to cut from the last for the Shichosonkai. In fact multi-member districts with S.N.T.V. were first introduced in national elections in 1900 when the first amendment to the election law was passed.

The Lower House election law was promulgated on February 11th, 1889, with the Meiji Imperial Constitution. After the first election in September 1890, the first congress was opened on November 29th, 1890. Since only those paying high taxes had suffrage, the majority of congress members were from the Minto group (Popular Party group) including the Jiyu-To (the Liberal Party, which is not a "direct" ancestor of the L.D.P.). These groups represented the squire class that paid most in taxes. Under the Meiji Imperial Constitution the prime minister was chosen by the Emperor, in effect the Hambatsu (feudal cliques) and aristocrats. The supporters of the government were a minority in the congress. The majority of the congress, who advocated tax reductions, was wildly opposed to the government, which advocated higher spending on armaments. Strife over this continued until the Sino-Japanese War of 1894–95. The strife calmed down for a while. The government succeeded in amending the election law at that time.

Many books on Japanese history, including high school textbooks inspected by the government, mention only the relaxation of the restriction of the suffrage according to the amount of tax paid or the administration of secret ballots.[12] But the first point to notice for our purpose here is that multi-member districts with single non-transferable voting began to be used.[13] Since there were many parties at that time, and party organization was not solid, there was almost no discussion in the congress about the S.N.T.V. rule, even though the disputes about the restriction of suffrage by tax paid or the independence of cities as districts were tough.[14] The strongest advocator of S.N.T.V., Kametaro Hayashida, was a bureaucrat who was very close to Hirobumi Ito, the first prime minister and a leader of the Hambatsu (feudal cliques). S.N.T.V. was slipped into the agenda by government supporters. The object was to intensify competition between the parties. From the beginning the object of S.N.T.V. was to prevent the formation of one large party.[15]

During the high inflation of World War I there were many riots, and the Emperor (in effect the Hambatsu group) had no choice but give the non-Hambatsu or the Popular Party group a chance to form a cabinet. Takashi Hara, the leader of the biggest party, the Rikken Seiyu Kai (the Friends of Constitutional Government Party, one of the descendants of the Jiyu-To) was chosen. He formed the first full-scale non-Hambatsu cabinet in 1918. The next year he succeed in introducing single-member districts.[16]

In the fourteenth election, which was held in 1920, the Rikken Seiyu Kai gained a great victory using single-member districts,[17] but the party broke up in 1924. After winning the fifteenth election, the Goken Sampa group (literally "Three Parties Supporting the Constitution") introduced universal manhood suffrage in 1925.[18] At this time the Goken Sampa introduced three- to five-member districts with S.N.T.V. The purpose was to enable each of three parties to win a seat in each district.[19]

After the universal male suffrage law in 1925, the reform movement in the Diet almost disappeared. S.N.T.V. continued to be used, without any strong reason for doing so, and the Japanese people became more and more accustomed to it. Japan went into World War II with this election rule.

One might think that the other problem, unfair apportionment, also appeared under the autocratic politics before World War II. In fact, such was not the case. As Tables 1–8 in Appendix 2 show, the apportionments before World War II were very fair, with the exception of Hokkaido, the frontier of Japan at that time. Since the election rules were changed so often, the apportionment became fair without any reapportionment. "Misapportionment" became a problem after World War II.

7

The electoral system after World War II: doing nothing and
becoming increasingly unfair

After World War II, Japan was occupied by the Allies, mainly the
United States. Under the U.S. occupation, many radical reforms,
including the *zaibatsu* dissolution of 1946[20] and the land reform of
1946 and 1947,[21] were brought about. Even the current constitution
was translated from English at that time. However, the electoral
system remained unchanged.

Restricted multi-voting, where each voter has fewer votes than
there are seats in the district, with prefecture-sized districts, was
used in the twenty-second election in 1946 under the 1945 election
law.[22] S.N.T.V. reappeared with districts of three to five members
at the twenty-third election in 1947. There were almost no major
changes except as regards women's suffrage and eligibility or the
right to become a candidate.

On October 9th, 1945, a professional diplomat, Kijuro
Shidehara, became the second prime minister since World War II.
People in the government felt that they needed to change the
election rule to please the Allied powers. The minister of home
affairs, Zenjiro Horikiri, who had been a bureaucrat in the Ministry
of Home Affairs, revealed the policy of amending the election law
at a cabinet meeting on October 11th. This policy included lower-
ing the age of suffrage and eligibility, women's suffrage and
eligibility, and prefecture-sized districts. In the afternoon of the
same day, the General Headquarters of the Allied Forces (G.H.Q.)
issued some directives changing the country's political economy;
these included women's suffrage and eligibility. Although the
policy was consistent with home minister Horikiri's policy, the
Ministry of Home Affairs, led by vice-minister Chiaki Saka, did not
want to be seen taking orders and hurried to prepare the agenda
for an amendment of the election law before G.H.Q.'s directive
was announced. According to Jichi Daigakko (1961), the idea was
to give women and the younger generation the vote and to have
prefecture-sized districts and restricted multi-voting.

On October 13th the cabinet decided the age for suffrage should
be twenty years, eligibility should be at twenty-five years and
women should have both rights. It decided on prefecture-sized
districts on October 20th and on the restricted multi-voting rule on
November 6th. The idea of the bureaucrats became the agenda of
the government in this short decision time.

Some people, including the leader of the Socialist Party, suggested a proportional representation system. But at an interview on November 1st the minister of home affairs, Zenjiro Horikiri, said that proportional representation would be premature. The concept had long been popular among Japanese academics, and the Lower House had approved an agenda for proportional representation as far back as 1909, though the House of Lords (the Upper House[23]) had rejected the agenda. It would be reasonable to assume that a former bureaucrat like Horikiri and bureaucrats at the Ministry of Home Affairs wanted to keep the power of political parties weak by using restricted multi-voting.

The results of the population survey of November 1st, 1945, became available on the 20th, and the Cabinet decided the apportionment on the 22nd. Some important points in the agenda of the new electoral law were the following:

1 Women had both the right to vote and the right to become candidates.
2 The age of suffrage was twenty years and eligibility was at twenty-five years. (Both had been lowered by five years.)
3 Some 466 seats were apportioned into prefectures. Hokkaido, Tokyo, Niigata, Aichi, Osaka, Hyogo and Fukuoka, which were allocated fifteen seats or more, were divided into two districts each.
4 Voters in one- to five-member districts would enter one name, the voters in six- to ten-member districts wrote in two names, and the voters in eleven- to fourteen-member districts wrote in three names.

This agenda can be considered very beneficial for the bureaucracy. Like S.N.T.V., restricted multi-voting does not provide a strong incentive to form big organized parties. With the single-member plurality rule one may need a big party to win. In a proportional representation system, one needs to form organized parties to make a list of candidates. Like S.N.T.V., the restricted multi-voting rule makes a campaign individualistic. Without any big organized party, the bureaucracy can have more power than the politicians.

The Lower House passed the agenda on December 11th and the Upper House (the House of the Lords at that time) on the 14th. The 1945 election law was promulgated on the 17th. This short decision-making time showed that both the government and the Diet were afraid of the intervention of G.H.Q.

9

On December 20th G.H.Q. asked for a translation of the law and received it on the 23rd. Some G.H.Q. members held a meeting on December 31st and January 2nd to discuss the new election law. Those attending the meeting, who were American, were not familiar with restricted multi-voting and the majority opposed it. But on January 4th, 1946, the Director of the Government Section (G.S.), Courtney Whitney, proposed that General Douglas MacArthur, the Supreme Commander for the Allied Powers (S.C.A.P.), should approve it. Americans at the top of G.H.Q. wanted to have a legitimate government established before the U.S.S.R. tried to intervene in Japanese politics. This incident is detailed to show that Americans at the top of G.H.Q. needed a quick election. Another reason may be that they believed the Occupation Purge of the same day, January 4th, was enough to bring about the democratization of Japan. G.H.Q. removed about 200,000 Japanese military, government and business leaders from their wartime positions and excluded them from public office.

MacArthur approved the electoral law. The twenty-second election, the first since World War II, was held on April 10th, 1946. The new election system prepared by bureaucrats was adopted without any important amendment. The reason would seem to be that both the government and the Diet were afraid of the intervention of G.H.Q.; and G.H.Q., in turn, was afraid of the intervention of the U.S.S.R. in Japanese politics. They were very much in a hurry to hold an election.

After the election a professional diplomat, Shigeru Yoshida, became prime minister with the support of the biggest party, the Japan Liberal Party, and the second biggest, the Japan Progressive Party.[24] In this election thirty-nine women[25] and five communists won seats in the Lower House. The reason for the former was thought to be that many voters, who could write two names on their ballot paper, had written a female name on the second line. The latter was believed to have happened because the prefecture-size districts, where an average of nine representatives were chosen, were too big.[26] The government was afraid of the advance of the Communist Party and advocated the three- to five-member districts with S.N.T.V. The government thought it would be difficult for communists to win one seat in a three- to five-member district even with S.N.T.V., and it was right. This agenda for changing the election rule was supported by MacArthur and on March 31st, 1947, the Diet passed the bill. Three- to five-member districts with

S.N.T.V. were adopted again. The post-war election rule became the same rule as that used before World War II because the government and G.H.Q. feared the advance of the Communist Party.

The 1947 electoral law followed the same rules as before World War II except for women's suffrage and eligibility.

Apportionment was still fair at this time. The other distinguishing characteristic of the current Japanese election system was not yet evident. According to the population data of April 1946, "The ratio of per representative population between most advantageous and disadvantageous" ("the ratio" later on)[27] was 1:1.25 between prefectures and 1:1.51 between districts. In 1950 the Lower House election law was rewritten and made part of the public office election law. But the election rule and apportionment were not changed, although the Diet added a clause to the effect that reapportionment should be undertaken after each census, taken every five years. As a result of the failure to reapportion, with the population data of the 1950 census the ratio became 1:1.55 between prefectures and 1:2.17 between districts. In 1954 the United States returned the island of Amami Gunto to Japan. The Diet did not take advantage of the opportunity for full reapportionment and just increased it by one representative assigned to Amami Gunto. According to the population data of the 1955 census, the ratio became 1:1.94 between prefectures and 1:2.68 between districts. In 1960 the census population data show the ratio as 1:2.39 between prefectures and 1:3.21 between districts. Finally, the results of the thirtieth election on November 21st, 1963, were submitted to the courts on the grounds that the ratio of voters at that time had become 1:3.55 between districts. The judicial decision of the Tokyo High Court was, unbelievably, that this unfair situation was constitutional, but in 1964 the first reapportionment was effected by adding nineteen representatives, and the ratio became 1:2.19 between districts on the population data of the 1960 census. Both the biggest party, the L.D.P., and the second biggest, the Japan Socialist Party (J.S.P.), had their basis in the rural areas, where the population was decreasing. Reapportionment has always been insufficient, from this amendment of 1964 to the current law of 1996.

Reapportionment was not brought about when Okinawa was returned to Japan by the United States. This was a good opportunity for reapportionment, but the Diet merely added five representatives and gave them to Okinawa. With the results of 1970

11

census population data, the ratio became 1:2.75 between prefectures and 1:4.83 between districts. The thirty-third election on December 10th in 1972 was contested in court because the ratio of voters became 1:4.99 between districts. Unbelievably, the judicial decision of the Tokyo High Court was that the election under this misapportionment was constitutional. But the Supreme Court ruled it unconstitutional, so the second reapportionment was done in July 1975. (The Supreme Court approved the result of the election itself and did not ask the Diet to hold another election. This lenient decision made the situation even worse. The Diet thought the apportionment problem was not such a severe one.) The Diet was increased by twenty representatives and the ratio became 1:2.06 between the prefectures and 1:2.92 between the districts, on the basis of the 1970 census population data.

This insufficient reapportionment brought the ratio to 1:2.32 between prefectures and 1:3.72 between districts, as judged from the population data of the 1975 census. The results of the thirty-fourth election, on December 5th, 1976, and the thirty-fifth, election on December 10th, 1979, were submitted to the courts because of this misapportionment. In both cases the plaintiffs could not get a judicial decision before the next elections. Japanese courts take too much time for such a simple problem. For the thirty-sixth election, on June 22nd, 1980, the judicial decision of the Supreme Court was that it was unconstitutional that the ratio of the voters per representative was 1:3.95 but the election itself was constitutional because of the short time lapse since the previous reapportionment. The Supreme Court hesitated to call for another election again. But the Diet could not amend the apportionment and the 1980 census showed that the ratio had become 1:2.41 between prefectures and 1:4.54 between districts. For the thirty-seventh election, on December 18th, 1983, the judicial decision of the Supreme Court was that the ratio of 1:4.41, given the figure for voters, was unconstitutional. In 1986 the Diet executed the third reapportionment, which increased the number of representatives in eight districts and reduced it in seven and brought the ratio down from 1:5.12 to 1:2.99 on the basis of the 1985 census. The reason for this insufficient reapportionment was that the judicial decision of the Supreme Court can be understood to mean that a ratio under 1:3 is constitutional. (Some of the judges said a ratio of more than 1:3 is unconstitutional, regardless of any other social conditions.) In fact, the judicial decisions concerning the thirty-

12

eighth election in 1986 and the thirty-ninth in 1990 were that they were constitutional. In 1992 the Diet executed the fourth reapportionment, which increased the apportionment in nine districts and decreased it in ten and changed the ratio from 3.38 to 2.72.

The biggest party, the L.D.P., is supported by farmers and fishermen. The second biggest party, the J.S.P., is supported by public employees who work for "the biggest industry in the rural areas."[28] It was natural that the reapportionments to reduce representation in rural areas were always insufficient. The judicial decisions of the Supreme Court were biased because all the judges had been chosen by L.D.P. prime ministers during that party's extremely long rule.[29] In fact, as mentioned before, this lopsided situation will continue even after the next electoral reform, this time by the Hosokawa, Hata and Murayama cabinets.

Three aspects of the Japanese electoral system

Multi-member districts with S.N.T.V. might have been introduced and reintroduced by the bureaucrats in order to reduce the power of political parties. The apportionment became worse and worse because nothing was done. But how should we evaluate these two characteristics of Japanese elections, "multi-member districts with S.N.T.V." and "unequal apportionment"? Is S.N.T.V. a bad characteristic because it was chosen under the influence of bureaucrats? Is unequal apportionment a good characteristic because the Supreme Court said it was constitutional and people kept moving to poorly apportioned areas? And how about the new election rule, which uses most standard election rules, single-member districts with plurality and a proportional representation system with a party-decided list all "together"? Is it good because it is the final compromise of the Japanese parties? Obviously we cannot evaluate these rules on the basis of their historical background. The following pages analyze and evaluate three aspects of the old and new Japanese electoral system.

A game theory study of Duverger's law

Multi-member districts with S.N.T.V. give better proportionality between votes and seats than a single-member plurality system. But some people, especially L.D.P. supporters, advocate single-member districts on the grounds that they will eventually

13

bring about a two-party system which will give Japan a guarantee of systematic political alternation. Their argument depends on Duverger's law, which advocates single-member districts plurality election rule favors a two-party system. In the election reform at the beginning of 1994, after the compromise with the centrist and leftist parties which supported a proportional representation system, the rightists succeeded in creating 300 single-member districts out of a total of 500 seats in the Lower House.

Will single-member districts necessarily result in a two-party system? We can easily cite examples of failure in India and Canada. Actually, the original Duverger's law is itself still disputed forty years since his "classic" was published in 1951. If Japan uses the new rule, will it have a two-party system at least in single-member districts?

This game theory study of Duverger's law is my proposal for the theoretical explanation of the original Duverger's law. Its implication is negative for the new Japanese election system.

The Liberal Democratic Party as a Coalition Government

Multi-member districts with S.N.T.V. would make the election more familiar to voters.[30] Compared with a proportional representative system, especially with a party-decided list of candidates, multi-member districts with S.N.T.V. make politicians more sensitive to voters.[31]

Wouldn't it work as a semi-proportional system? It might work similarly to Ireland's system, in which votes for individuals are taken into account. As Cox (1991) shows theoretically, the result of S.N.T.V. is very similar to the result of the d'Hondt (Jefferson) method, or, since big parties sometimes make mistakes, the result is close to the result of the Sainte Lagüe (Webster) method which is more proportional than the d'Hondt method, as Balinski and Young (1982) show. Lijphart et al. (1986), whose idea of proportionality is the d'Hondt type, present and criticize the fact that multi-member districts with S.N.T.V. do not keep seats and votes in porportion, but the first and the second cases they offer are equivalent to the result of the Sainte Lagüe method because of the "mistake" of the L.D.P.

The L.D.P. itself might be just a coalition government under a semi-proportional system. Ishikawa (1984) has said:

14

Bigger parties in Japan have factions. Especially in the L.D.P., each faction has its own office, its own accounting system, and its own councillors, just like a party. In fact, the L.D.P. government is nothing but a coalition government of factions.

Factions may not be a bossism product and L.D.P. may be a coalition of parties which are called "factions". This hypothesis can be proved by showing that the L.D.P. works according to the same logic as that by which European coalition governments work. The Schofield and Laver (1985, 1987) type of bargaining set (or cooperative game theory) model that explains the coalition governments in Europe may also work and explain outcomes in Japan. The old Japanese electoral rule, multi-member districts with single non-transferable voting, might be considered a semi-proportional representation system that makes politicians sensitive to the voters, if, in the final stage of the election, a cabinet formation is similar to the European ones. The L.D.P. might be just a coalition "group" under that system.

The economic effect of the apportionment of representatives

The best known distortion caused by elections is the political business cycle. But Japanese political business cycles are considered as "surf-riding". The essays of Inoguchi (1983) or Wada (1985), which depend on Frey and Schneider type empirical work or theoretically Nordhaus (1975) type pre-rational expectations opportunistic models, do not find distortions in budgetory or monetary policy caused by politics related to elections. Neither do more sophisticated works like Alesina and Roubini (1990) or Ito (1989). The Japanese government just tried to hold an election in a good economic situation or just tried to "ride the surf".

Are there no distortions in the budget caused by elections in Japan? Although we can find almost no distortion by election "date", there is a big distortion by misapportionment, as we have seen. The L.D.P. clearly used this biased system to stay in power.[32] This biased system reinforced "the stable L.D.P. politics". Anyone can keep in power by means of such misapportionment. Nevertheless, the nation's demand for a reapportionment of representatives is still not strong.

As we have seen, in July 1985 the Supreme Court handed down the decision that the apportionment where the biggest ratio of *per capita* representatives between the districts was 1:4.41 is against the constitution. The newspaper *Minami-nippon-shinbun* criticized it, saying in a headline: "Supreme Court tries to reduce our political power and pursues depopulation,"[33] even though the decision of the Supreme Court was not to enforce the reallocation of the unfair apportionment. Unfortunately the view of this local newspaper is supported by some leading scholars[34] and the decisions of the Supreme Court can be understood as holding that the biggest ratio of *per capita* representatives between the districts, 1:3, is constitutional. This third analysis, of the economic effect of the apportionment of representatives, indicates that such an unequal apportionment makes the welfare of even the people who have more representatives worse than under an ideal apportionment.

2

A GAME THEORY ANALYSIS OF DUVERGER'S LAW

Introduction

Japan will soon start to use a new election rule. The Diet has passed a new law providing that 300 Lower House members will be chosen by a single-member district plurality system and 200 will be chosen separately by proportional representation with a party-decided list of candidates. This outcome is the result of a simple compromise between the L.D.P. and the Ozawa group, which support a single-member district plurality system, and the anti-L.D.P. parties, which support a proportional representation system.

Supporters of single-member districts argue that they will bring about a two-party system which will give Japan a guarantee of systematic political alternation. Their argument depends on Duverger's law, which implies that single-member districts with a plurality election rule will favor a two-party system.

Duverger's law, which is usually understood to say that single-member district plurality voting systems favor a two-party system, may be the most famous and disputed "law" in political science. The disputes have continued for at least forty years since Duverger's classic work (1951) appeared, and they started even before Duverger. (See Riker 1982, 1986 for the history.) Does Duverger's law work? Does a single-member district plurality voting system always lead to a two-party system? Unfortunately Duverger's law is not always supported by the empirical data. Famous counter-examples are Canada and India. Canada has three parties, India has one big party and an enormous number of small parties. Even England has a non-negligible third party. Only the United States might be a supporting example of Duverger's law

17

among big countries. Should we just throw away Duverger's law? Maybe not. Because it contains a simple and interesting intuition.

Let us see the intuition given by Duverger himself. Duverger (1951, p. 224) suggests two reasons why single-member district plurality voting systems favor a two-party system. One is the result of the "fusion" (or an alliance very like fusion) of the weak parties, and the other is the "elimination" of weak parties by the voters, by which he means that the voters gradually desert the weak parties on the grounds that they have no chance of winning. Many political scientists study Duverger's law in the context of "rationality". It would be rational for the weak parties to merge rather than to get nothing. It would be rational for the voters not to vote for parties which have no chance of winning.

Since empirically Duverger's law does not always work, we should check this simple intuition. Why does the real world sometimes work as Duverger predicted and sometimes not? Such theoretical checks on intuition are always useful. Remember the Phillips curve in economics. In the 1950s or 1960s economists may have believed in a stable trade-off ratio between unemployment and inflation. This relationship was broken in the 1970s. But theoretical study gave economists a deeper understanding of "expectations". Now we know some conditions where we may have a beautiful Phillips curve and others where we will not have such a curve.

Duverger's law may work in some circumstances. Does it work in the circumstance of Japan? Can Japan's new election system have a two-party basis, at least in the single-member district with plurality part of the new Japanese system? Theoretical analysis is needed to answer these questions.

Duverger (1951, 1986) and others, including Riker (1982, 1986) and Sartori (1976, 1986), have been interested in explaining the number of political parties. Their reasoning depends on the rationality of the voters or the parties. But, strictly speaking, formal theorists of Duverger's law talk mainly about the number of candidates in each district and not about the number of parties itself. So, in our discussion, we focus mainly on the number of candidates in each single-member district under the plurality voting system.

One way of explaining Duverger's law is to study entry and entry deterrence in a Hotelling and Downs type position-selecting model. Brams and Straffin (1982), Palfrey (1984), Greenberg and

Shepsle (1987), Shepsle and Cohen (1990), Feddersen *et al.* (1990) and Weber (1990, forthcoming) are examples of this type of approach. This approach also depends on the assumption of the "rationality" of the candidate for winning the election, but the ideas behind the reasoning may be slightly different from Duverger's original reasoning. Their concern seems to be whether two candidates could deter the third candidate from entering the race by changing their ideological positions. A Hotelling and Downs type position-selecting model would be suitable for a presidential system like the one in the United States where each candidate for congress can choose his or her ideological or political position to maximize his or her own chances of victory.[1] But it might not be suitable for a parliamentary system, where a party leader must decide the party's ideological or political position when forming a cabinet, and where the party's candidate in each district is constrained by the party position. Since the countries where the applicability of Duverger's law is doubtful[2] use a parliamentary system, we may have to adopt other types of models to study Duverger's law. Japan also uses a parliamentary system.

Another popular way to study Duverger's law is by assuming "voters' rationality" and the likelihood of strategic voting. In multi-candidate elections, voters may not vote for their most preferred candidate when they think the possibility of the most preferred candidate's winning is slight. This may eliminate weak parties as Duverger expected when he wrote about the "elimination effect".

Riker (1976) introduced the notions of sophisticated voting[3] and disillusioned voting,[4] and used them to analyze the dynamics of the number of political parties. His model is interesting, but some of his assumptions may be arbitrary. This seems especially true where, in order to explain the Indian situation (one big party competes with many small parties), Riker assumed that the social axis of ideology restricts the direction of change of individuals' support. Palfrey (1989), Myerson and Weber (1993) and Cox (1994) used sophisticated game theory with the assumption of rational voters and incomplete information about the distribution of other voters' preferences to explain Duverger's law.

Some voters vote strategically in the real world. In a multi-candidate election they do not vote for their most preferred candidate when they think the possibility of the most preferred candidate's winning is low. They may try to get the second best candidate elected. But is strategic voting the main support for

Duverger's law? It may not be a strong enough factor for the elimination of the third party. Japan uses single-member district plurality election for prefectual governor, city mayor and the Upper House general election in rural areas and the Upper House filling-vacancy election. Usually in such elections the J.C.P., in addition to the L.D.P. and the J.S.P., has a candidate and continues to retain a significant number of votes, though there is almost no possibility of its candidate winning. It is not seldom the case that if all the J.C.P.'s supporters had voted for the J.S.P. candidate the latter would have won. But in fact the L.D.P. candidate won. If voters are fully rational, J.C.P. supporters should vote for the J.S.P. because they may have single-peaked preferences and may not want to use their votes ineffectively for the final choice of their district. The rational voter should try to prevent the victory of his or her least preferred candidate.

A more important problem might be that candidates who know they will be defeated often do not exit from the electoral com-petition. Candidates must have more information and should be more rational than voters. If voters are rational, why don't candi-dates who will be defeated exit? In the models, like Palfrey (1989) or Myerson and Weber (1993), a candidate is just an alternative. Voters play an election game strategically, but candidates do not. Their voters are rational, but the candidates are not. We should study candidates' rationality before voters' rationality.

To run or to exit is the basic strategic choice of candidates in the election game. This is a more decisive strategy for the candidates than position selecting is. The result of this game gives the number of candidates who run. It directly shows whether Duverger's law works or not. However, it has not been studied very much, even though many people, including Riker (1982, p. 761; 1986, p. 33) and Shepsle (1991, p. 62), have mentioned it along with strategic voting. One exception I know of is Humes (1990). But he just gives some results in some arbitrary voters' distributions and his model may have some problems as a theoretical model. This seems to be especially the case regarding his assumption No. 6, "if a political party is going to lose the next election with certainty, it prefers not expending effort of the election (withdrawing) to expending effort on the election." If we accepted this assumption we should always have only one candidate, except in the knife-edge case, because in Hume's model the distribution of voters is common knowledge. All possible candidates know the distribution of voters, and they also know that other people know it. They can solve the game and know who will win.

We should understand the exit of a candidate as an implicit alliance with another candidate rather than as a means of saving effort on the part of the candidate who exits. If exit is just for cost saving, it should easily occur. Exit should occur even in circumstances where there is some possibility of winning, if the cost is more than the expected benefit of winning. In fact, exit means that a candidate gives his or her supporting votes to other candidates. So it may not always occur. It is very understandable that candidates may not agree or be able to decide who should exit and give his or her supporting vote to others. Therefore, people stand for election not only in the case where winning is possible but also sometimes when they know they cannot win. Exit may depend on the conditions. Let us study this in our game theory model.

This mechanism, exit, is the only hope of Duverger's law working in Japan to give Japan a two-party system under the new election rule. Since Japan has a parliamentary system, candidates cannot adopt another strategy such as changing their ideological position. From past data we cannot expect the rationality of the voters or strategic voting to eliminate the third party. If exit or implicit alliance does not work, Japan may not obtain a two-party system even in a single-member district part of the new system.

Model

Let us set up our model. Our focal point is a local district, and the game is played there.

The setting

1 The policy space is one-dimensional. This might be a traditional assumption for simplicity and many position-selecting models adopt it. It might not be so unrealistic, because at least five main Japanese parties, the L.D.P., the Democratic Socialist Party (D.S.P.), the Clean Government Party (C.G.P. or Komei-to), the J.S.P. and the J.C.P. can be considered as occupying different points along one ideological continuum. (See Iwai 1988, p. 113.)
2 The election rule is single-member district plurality where a candidate wins an election if and only if he or she gains more

21

votes than any other candidate. For convenience, it is assumed that ties do not occur.

Candidates

1 There are three nationwide parties and each has one candidate, A, B and C, in this district. Each party's position is nationally decided and its candidate in this district must have the same position as the national party. For simplicity no two parties share the same position in the policy space. Three-party models are used by many formal theorists, including Riker (1976), Palfrey (1989) and Humes (1990). It may be natural to start to study multi-party systems from the simplest assumption about them. It might also be enough to imagine the Japanese situation. For analyzing single-member districts we may be able to distinguish three groups: (1) rightist – L.D.P, (2) centrist – D.S.P. and C.G.P. (Komei-to) with J.R.P. (Ozawa faction) and Japan New Party (J.N.P., Hosokawa's party),[5] (3) leftist – J.S.P.[6]

2 A candidate in this district has two strategies, to run or to exit.

3 The cost of running is assumed to be 0. Our results will hold for a small negative cost (or a small benefit) of running, but for simplicity we assume there is no cost or benefit. Contrary to the assumptions of some other authors, including Riker (1982, p. 761; 1986, p. 33) and Shepsle (1991, p. 62), we are assuming that running would be beneficial to the party because of its advertisement value and the total cost might be 0. This might be especially true if there were public support for the candidate. This assumption is supported by the fact that in Japan, in order to reduce the number of frivolous candidates, the candidates are asked to deposit some money. The fact that there is a need to increase the deposit suggests that there is either no cost or actual positive benefit to a candidate in running. Under the new Japanese election system, the proportional representation part of the system reinforces the benefits of running in the single-member district part of the system. It is a good campaign strategy for the proportional representation part of the election to run candidates for the single-member district part. For example, in the United States, running for the House of Representatives on a party ticket may help the presidential election or senatorial election candidates of that party even where there is almost no chance of the candidate winning in his or her own district.

22

4 Each candidate has single-peaked preferences. The pay-off for the candidate depends on the final winner's position. It is a very natural assumption that, if there is no chance of they themselves winning, conservatives prefer socialists winning to communists winning and that communists prefer socialists winning to conservatives winning. In multi-candidate elections it would be very strange if we assumed all-or-nothing preferences. Nor would it be sensible to assume that conservatives prefer communists winning to socialists winning in the case where they have no chance of winning themselves. I assume that implicit alliances between A and B or B and C are possible but alliances between A and C are impossible.[7]

Voters

1 Each voter has single-peaked preferences.
2 Voters always vote sincerely. With this assumption voters are not players in our game. Since at least many Japanese voters do not vote strategically, as we saw before, this assumption would be plausible.

Solution

"Trembling hand" perfect equilibria are our solution. To assume trembling hand perfect equilibria means assuming there is a small possibility that players may make mistakes. Do political parties make some mistakes? Sure, they do. For example, in Japanese multi-member district elections the L.D.P. often has more candidates than the number of seats allocated to a particular district and the J.S.P. sometimes fails to field a candidate even though there is considered to be a significant chance of winning. If you do not want to use trembling hand perfect equilibria, assume that there are small total benefits if candidates run. In such cases Nash equilibria are enough to get the same solutions.

Model solving

Because of the assumption of single-peaked voters' preferences, voters can be divided into four groups depending on their preferences. (For simplicity, let us assume there is no indifferent case.)

1	Group α	$A \succ B \succ C$
2	Group $\beta\alpha$	$B \succ A \succ C$
3	Group $\beta\gamma$	$B \succ C \succ A$
4	Group γ	$C \succ B \succ A$

The curved inequality sign "$\succ$" means "is preferred to". Since we assume single-peaked voters' preferences, there is no one who prefers A to C and C to B (A$\succ$C$\succ$B), or C to A and A to B (C$\succ$A$\succ$B). Let us call the number of voters in each group #α, #$\beta\alpha$, #$\beta\gamma$ and #γ and also #β=#$\beta\alpha$+#$\beta\gamma$.

In order to solve our game, we must divide the game into some cases. According to the combination of the relative sizes of each group, our game is divided into only eight cases, as follows.

(Three run)	(A vs. B)	(A vs. C)	(B vs. C)
1 #α>#β,#γ:	#α>#β+#γ;	#α+#$\beta\alpha$>#$\beta\gamma$+#γ;	#α+#β>#γ.
2 #α>#β,#γ:	#α<#β+#γ;	#α+#$\beta\alpha$>#$\beta\gamma$+#γ;	#α+#β>#γ.
3 #α>#β,#γ:	#α<#β+#γ;	#α+#$\beta\alpha$<#$\beta\gamma$+#γ;	#α+#β>#γ.
4 #β>#α,#γ:	#α<#β+#γ;	#α+#$\beta\alpha$>#$\beta\gamma$+#γ;	#α+#β>#γ.
5 #β>#α,#γ:	#α<#β+#γ;	#α+#$\beta\alpha$<#$\beta\gamma$+#γ;	#α+#β>#γ.
6 #γ>#α,#β:	#α<#β+#γ;	#α+#$\beta\alpha$>#$\beta\gamma$+#γ;	#α+#β>#γ.
7 #γ>#α,#β:	#α<#β+#γ;	#α+#$\beta\alpha$<#$\beta\gamma$+#γ;	#α+#β>#γ.
8 #γ>#α,#β:	#α<#β+#γ;	#α+#$\beta\alpha$<#$\beta\gamma$+#γ;	#α+#β<#γ.

In our game a voter does not vote strategically but votes sincerely for the candidate whom he or she likes most among the running candidates. So the first inequality in each case shows who will win the election when all three run, because it shows who has the most supporters. The second inequality in each case shows who would win the election as between A and B, because only group α, whose preference is $A \succ B \succ C$, vote for A and group β, whose preference is $B \succ A \succ C$ or $B \succ C \succ A$, and group γ, whose preference is $C \succ B \succ A$, vote for B. Again, since we assume single-peaked preferences, there is no one whose preference is $A \succ C \succ B$ or $C \succ A \succ B$. This inequality shows which is greater, #α or #β+#γ, that is, A's votes or B's votes. The third inequality shows who would win the election as between A and C, and the last shows who would win the election as between B and C.

Because of the assumption of single-peakedness of the candidates the game is solved as shown in Tables 28 to 37.

The intuition behind each case would be as follows. In case 1, as Table 28 shows, since A is dominant, both B and C run, A's

24

mistake having given them a rare chance. If A runs, there is no chance of B or C winning (A is dominant), so B and C can run anyway. In case 2, as Table 29 shows, in order to beat A, who has the most support, C, who has no chance if B runs, is implicitly forced to exit in order to help B win. (B's winning is the second best choice for C, next to him or herself winning, because of the single-peaked preference assumption of the candidates.) To solve case 3, we need an extra assumption about candidate B's preferences. Let us call the case where candidate B prefers A's winning to C's winning "case 3-1" and the case where B prefers C's winning to A's winning "case 3-2". In case 3-1, since B prefers A to C, as Table 30 shows, B can run anyway. C will be implicitly forced to cooperate because of his or her single-peaked preference. In case 3-2, as Table 31 shows, without a suitable focal point, the crash of the "chicken" game[8] might occur. Both B and C would refuse to cooperate (exit) and A, which is least preferred by both B and C, might win. If the Condorcet winner, which means the party that will win in all pairwise races, should become a focal point, C would exit and B would win. In case 4, as Table 32 shows, since B is too strong, both A and C run, having a rare chance to win.[9] Cases 5, 6-1, 6-2, 7 and 8 are the mirror images of cases 4, 3-2, 3-1, 2 and 1, respectively. If we exchange group α and group γ in case 5, it is exactly the same as case 4. Candidate C in case 5 plays like candidate A in case 4 and candidate A in case 5 plays like candidate C in case 4.

We get two theorems from the tables.

1 *Negative theorem.* Exit, which means implicit alliance, occurs only if the Condorcet winner is not the biggest party. This theorem tells us we can seldom expect two candidates' election in our situation. Duverger's law does not work well.

2 *Positive theorem.* Except for the case of a chicken game without a suitable focal point, the Condorcet winner always wins the election in the equilibrium.[10]

Concluding remarks

Duverger (1951, p. 224) suggests two reasons for his law: the fusion (or an alliance very like fusion) of the weak parties, and the elimination by voters of weak parties. Many formal theorists study the second reason, the rationality of voters, in the context of strategic voting. But the first reason, the rationality of candidates, is not studied so much. Most theorists study the rationality of candidates mainly from the viewpoint of their position-selecting strategy. The story of our model fits the first reason of Duverger himself and shows that the first reason does not always work.

According to our model, we can say that, even though Japan chose a single-member district plurality system, it may be difficult to get a two-party system. As the past data show, "rationality of the voters" or strategic voting is not strong enough to eliminate the third party. Since Japan has a parliamentary system where independence for an individual candidate is not easy, we cannot rely on the "rationality of candidates" to choose ideological or policy positions and thereby to deter the third party. The only hope of making Duverger's law work in Japan's new system was that "the rationality of candidates" would lead them to exit from the election and form an implicit alliance. But, as our model shows, this mechanism does not necessarily work.

In early 1994 the Diet passed a law creating an electoral system where 300 of the members are chosen by a single-member district plurality system and the remaining 200 are chosen separately by proportional representation. Under this arrangement the proportional representation part of the new system reinforces the benefits of running for the single-member district part. The alliance of L.D.P. oppositions would therefore become much more difficult. Since cooperation between the centrist and the leftist would be difficult, the L.D.P. might win almost all single-member districts. I would particularly fear the crash of the chicken game shown in case 4-2. The L.D.P. might win a more than proportional number of seats because of a chicken game crash of the opposition parties.

A single-member plurality election will not necessarily bring the two-party system that has been seen as the biggest merit of the new system. Because of the proportional representation element of the new system, Japan will never have a two-party system even in the single-member district with plurality part. The arrangement will just bring about a terribly distorted multi-party system.

We studied a mechanism of Duverger's law in the context of Japan's new election rule and showed that the single-member plurality election will not necessarily bring about a two-party system. This result may be universal: though strategic voting exists all over the world,[11] it is not strong enough by itself to make Duverger's law work. A presidential system like that of the United

26

States, where each candidate for congress can freely choose his or her position just for his or her own victory, may result in a two-party system. But, as we have seen, the prime ministership and single-member districts with a plurality system do not necessarily result in a two-party system. Without a guarantee of systematic alternation between two political parties, proportional represent-ation or multi-member districts with S.N.T.V. may be superior to single-member districts with a plurality system. Under the multi-party system the multi-member districts with S.N.T.V. guarantee proportionality more than single-member districts with a plurality system would. From this point of view, multi-member districts with S.N.T.V. may be superior to one of the most common election rules, single-member districts with plurality.

3

THE LIBERAL
DEMOCRATIC PARTY AS A
COALITION GOVERNMENT

Introduction

From its establishment in 1955 to the split of the Ozawa faction in 1993, the Liberal Democratic Party (L.D.P.) has always been the Japanese government's ruling party by itself.[1] The L.D.P. has been called a predominant party.[2] However, there is a consensus among researchers that the L.D.P. is not a single party but a coalition of different factions.[3] Each faction in the L.D.P. has its own office, its own accounts system, and its own councillors as if it were a party. Ishikawa said[4] that Japanese politics should be analyzed from the viewpoint of the L.D.P. as a coalition of different factions. This is appropriate, in part because the size of the L.D.P. factions is almost the same as the size of the opposition parties. (See Tables 38 to 40.)

In the Lower House elections under the old system, almost all constituencies chose between three to five legislators, which means that the L.D.P. usually had more than one candidate in each district. Under the single non-transferable voting (S.N.T.V.) rule the L.D.P. candidates compete for the same conservative voters,[5] hence it was very difficult for the party to support all the L.D.P. candidates. Therefore usually each L.D.P. candidate ran for the election only with the support of his or her own faction. It was not unusual for a new conservative candidate to run as an independent, not as an L.D.P. candidate, and after the election to join the L.D.P. The leader of the faction supported candidates who made his faction larger and provided a better chance of the leader winning the contest for the L.D.P. governor (party leader) or the prime ministership. L.D.P. governments may have been coalition governments under the multi-member districts with the single non-transferable voting or a "semi-proportional representation" system.[6]

The factions of the L.D.P. have been most prominent and

28

competitive during the election of the L.D.P. governor (party leader) and his cabinet formation. Many researchers studying this area have noticed that the mechanism of its coordination has changed over the years. Tominomori (1992, p. 25) divides the L.D.P. ruling years into two periods, before 1979 and after 1980, and lists three new phenomena in the second period.

The first phenomenon is the continuance of the same L.D.P. policies after 1980 even with the change of governor. Tominomori (1992, p. 32) says that before choosing Ohira in 1978 the new governor, using catch phrases, criticized the past governor's politics. But after 1980 there was no clear criticism of the incumbent governor.

The second phenomenon is the change in the method of choosing the governor. Tominomori (1992, p. 27) says that pre-1978 elections resembled a capture style while post-1980 elections have resembled an abdication style. He describes the two time periods in this way because before 1978 there usually were real elections.[7] But since 1980 there has been coordination among the factions before the election.

The third phenomenon is a division of the power and the proportional sharing of the portfolios of the cabinet after 1970. Tominomori (1992, p. 29) says that, before 1970, some factions did not support the cabinet. But after 1970 in most cases all factions had member(s) in the cabinet.

Since this third phenomenon was observed earlier than the other two and can be analyzed quantitatively, many researchers have mentioned it.[8] Inoguchi (1990, 1991a, b) characterized the change as a change from minimum winning coalition[9] to wall-to-wall coalition. Inoguchi (1991a) says that the principle of all factions joining the whole coalition cabinet has been the norm even though there was stiff competition between the factions during the late 1970s.

Why has such a cooperative structure been formed? Kanazashi (1989) calls it a wise arrangement for stability of the political power. But he does not explain the mechanics of the stabilization.

Yoda (1985) lists three explanations of the mechanism. First, the disappearance of the animosities between the politicians who had previously been bureaucrats, on the one hand, and the politicians who started out as politicians on the other. After World War II, during the Occupation Purge, it was easy for bureaucrats to become representatives, because the old politicians had been purged. Prime minister Shigeru Yoshida secured many candidates who were former bureaucrats for his faction. Yoshida's faction and its descendant factions had more former bureaucrats than other factions. But Yoda's first explanation is not persuasive, because only Yoshida's faction and its descendant factions had this character and its coalition partners did not have more past bureaucrats than other factions.

His second explanation is the bureaucratization of the organization of the L.D.P. However, this is not a reason but the result of the stabilized system of cooperative organization.

The third reason Yoda gives is the unanimous support for the governor within the L.D.P. organization during a time when it seems to have less political power. But this third reason may not be persuasive if one observes the supporting ratio of the L.D.P. and the behavior of its factions. L.D.P. factions do not necessarily support the governor when the supporting ratio of the L.D.P. is low.

Inoguchi (1990) uses the bandwagon effect of the predominant faction for his explanation of the stability of the wall-to-wall coalition. That is, other smaller factions joined the predominant faction to support its candidate. But it may be irrational for the predominant faction to want a bandwagon effect, because the number of cabinet posts is limited and some of them may have to be given to smaller factions.

Kohno (1991, 1992) says that this is an example of a repeated game and a nested game. But he did not explain the "change" in a game theory perspective.

I think the reason for the change from the minimum winning coalition type of cabinet formation to the wall-to-wall type is the change in the "rules of the game". In other words, during the 1970s and 1980s the policy stance of the opposition parties has come closer to that of the L.D.P. than before. In the 1960s or early 1970s one needed just half of the L.D.P. representatives' support to become prime minister, because no one could imagine a coalition between L.D.P. factions and the opposition parties. Losing factions also supported the winner of the race for the L.D.P. governor (party leader) in the congress election to choose the prime minister. So a minimum winning coalition was reasonable. But in the late 1970s or 1980s the L.D.P. factions were more ready to accept a coalition with the opposition parties. There was a change in the political climate.

Some of the factions within the L.D.P. may have used the threat to leave the L.D.P. and form a new coalition with other parties to gain some (extra) cabinet positions. After the late 1970s, at the local government level, we often see a prefectural governor supported by the L.D.P., the Democratic Socialist Party (D.S.P.) and the Clean Government Party (C.G.P.) or sometimes by the L.D.P., the D.S.P., the C.G.P. and the Japan Socialist Party (J.S.P.), or in rare cases by all the parties. Sometimes the L.D.P. splits into different factions which combine with opposition parties and support different candidates for governor. This could have been the case during the struggle for the prime ministership "between two L.D.P. members" in the Diet in November 1979 or at the time of the "Nikaido happening" in October 1984, when the opposition parties tried to make the former vice-governor of the L.D.P. their candidate for prime minister. In 1993 the Ozawa faction finally split from the L.D.P. and formed a coalition government with opposition parties. Since 1994 Japan has been governed by a coalition of the L.D.P. and the J.S.P. Coalition governments of different parties did not emerge until 1993, but at the latest by the end of the 1970s the factions of the L.D.P. might have played a game of threatening to form a coalition with parties outside the L.D.P.

The new rules of the game in the Diet after the end of the 1970s may be similar to the "rule" European coalition governments follow under proportional representation systems. Schofield and Laver (1985, 1987) found that the game of forming coalition governments in some European countries can be seen as bargaining with "threats" to win some (extra) cabinet positions. The L.D.P. was a coalition government of factions under a semi-proportional representation system and thus akin to the European coalition governments under proportional representation systems. The L.D.P.'s ostensible cooperative structure may have been seen to be due to threats by factions to form coalition governments with parties outside the L.D.P.

Let us move on to a general way of showing how a "coalition" is formed in bargaining by factions using "threats".

If faction i could leave out faction j and form a new coalition with other factions and opposition parties and get more cabinet seats, faction i would lodge an "objection" to faction j. On the other hand, if faction j could form another coalition without faction i and give the same or more seats to its partners, faction j would lodge a "counter-objection". For the stability of the coalition (L.D.P.) and

31

the portfolio of cabinet seats, there should be no "objection" or, if there are, all "objections" should be matched by "counter-objections". Actually the portfolios which satisfy this condition constitute what is defined as a "B1 bargaining set".

If we were to use a "group of factions J" instead of "faction j", it would be defined as a "B2 bargaining set". Since "group of factions J" could be "a faction j", the requirement of a B2 bargaining set is stricter than for a B1 bargaining set. Therefore this set belongs to the B1 bargaining set.

Let me illustrate this notion with the example of Finland in March 1970 given by Schofield (1982). The situation of the Finnish Diet was as follows. (Let us use symbols instead of the parties' names to make the illustration simple.)

Symbol	A	B	C	D	E	F	G	Total
Seats	51	37	36	12	8	37	18	199

Parties A, B, C, D and E formed a coalition and their total seats numbered 144. The B2 bargaining set is predicted as follows.

1 Suppose Party A's portfolio was less than one-third ($x_A < \frac{1}{3}$). Then A can form a winning coalition with FG, giving F and G one-third each. To counter BCDE with ninety-three seats needs either F or G. But the excess of BCDE, which is x_A, is less than one-third and so there is no counter. Hence, if portfolio x belongs to the B2 bargaining set, A's portfolio must be equal to or bigger than one-third ($x \in B_2 \rightarrow x_A \geq \frac{1}{3}$).

2 Let us check B's portfolio, x_B. Since B with C is pivotal to the ABCDE coalition, we may consider an objection by B with C against ADE. Suppose then that B objects with CFG to ADE. To counter ADE (with seventy-one seats) needs either C or F. If $3x_B + 2x_C < 1$, then B may offer more than $x_B + x_C$ to both C and F and make its new portfolio bigger than the old portfolio (x_B). The excess of ADE is $x_B + x_C$ and so ADE has no counter with either C or F, because B gave more than $x_B + x_C$ to each of them. Hence $x \in B_2 \rightarrow 3x_B + 2x_C \geq 1$.

3 Since C with B is pivotal to the ABCDE coalition, from the same logic as in (2), we can say, $x \in B_2 \rightarrow 2x_B + 3x_C \geq 1$.

4 Consider now objections by the other pivotal sub-groups, BD, BE, CD. For $x \in B_2$ we find the following:

(BD against ACE) $4x_B + 3x_D \geq 1$
$3x_B + 4x_D \geq 1$

(BE against ACD) $4x_B + 3x_E \geq 1$

$3x_B + 4x_E \geq 1$

(CD against ABE) $4x_C + 3x_D \geq 1$

$3x_C + 4x_D \geq 1$

Since the total portfolio is eighteen in the Finnish cabinet, from these restrictions we can predict a portfolio which is very close to the actual outcome.[10]

Symbol	A	B	C	D	E	Total
B2 bargaining set	6	5	4	2	1	18
Actual	5	5	4	2	2	18

The B2 bargaining set gives us insight and often predictions, but sometimes this set is empty. Let me illustrate an empty set with the example of Finland in March 1962 given by Schofield (1982). The situation in the Finnish Diet was as follows.

Symbol	A	B	C	D	E	F	G	Total
Seats	53	32	14	14	47	38	2	200

Parties A, B, C and D formed a coalition and their total number of seats was 113. The B2 bargaining set is predicted as follows.

1 Suppose $x_A < \frac{1}{2}$. Then A objects to BCD by giving half to E. Since BCD need E to counter, they cannot counter A.

$$x \in B_2 \rightarrow x_A \geq \frac{1}{2}$$

2 Suppose $x_B < \frac{1}{3}$. Then B objects to ACD by giving a third to E and F. Since ACD needs either E or F, but their excess is less than a third,

$$x \in B_2 \rightarrow x_B \geq \frac{1}{3}$$

3 Suppose $x_C < \frac{1}{4}$. Then C objects to ABD by giving a quarter each to E, F and G. ABD can counter with either E or F or G, but the excess is insufficient for a counter.

$$x \in B_2 \rightarrow x_C \geq \frac{1}{4}$$

4 Similarly,

$$x \in B_2 \rightarrow x_D \geq \frac{1}{4}$$

Since $\frac{1}{2} + \frac{1}{3} + \frac{1}{4} + \frac{1}{4} > 1$, the B2 bargaining set is empty. Since the B1 bargaining set is often too big to give a useful prediction, Schofield (1978) introduced a new notion called the B* bargaining set, which is included in the B1 bargaining set, includes the B2 bargaining set and is always non-empty. The exact mathematical definition and the proof of the characteristics is not straight-forward,[11] but the idea is "the situation where everyone has an objection without having a counter-objection." The B* bargaining set predicts portfolio (5, 3, 2, 2), which was the actual outcome in this case.

Schofield and Laver (1985, 1987) used another notion called the "Kernel". The idea is as follows. If there is a difference between the total pay-off of the current coalition, except faction j's pay-off, and the total pay-off of another potential coalition that includes faction i and does not include faction j, faction i feels that amount of a "regret" or has that amount of "excess demand". This "regret" changes according to what the potential coalition is, but we can find the "maximum regret" or "maximum excess demand" for each faction. For a stable coalition or portfolio, according to the model of the kernel, the outcome must equalize everyone's "maximum regret" by adjusting the portfolio. This is the intuition of the kernel. The kernel does not predict the real portfolio well in the case of European countries (Schofield and Laver 1985, 1987), but I will check it in Japanese cases.

Both the bargaining set and the kernel are famous notions of cooperative game theory and we can see the mathematical defini-tions in the textbooks of game theory by Owen (1982) and Shubik (1982), among others.[12] They are very good for showing the "power" in the game. Let us assume a parliament consisting of parties A, B and C. Party A has twenty members and both party B and party C have forty members each. Is party A's bargaining power a half of B's or C's? Maybe not. In forming a majority their power would be the same. If A and B formed a coalition their pay-off would be the same. Every party needs a partner to get a majority. As with a bargaining game player, all parties' powers are the same. Both the bargaining set and the kernel predict not proportional pay-offs but equal pay-offs. This prediction is plausible.

Schofield and Laver (1985, 1987) use the notion of the bargain-ing set and the kernel to analyze European coalition governments. According to the empirical work of Schofield and Laver (1985, 1987), countries with one "policy dimension" usually have a proportional portfolio, and countries with more than two policy dimensions have the portfolio in the bargaining set. It would be understandable that one could bargain more freely without the restriction of single strong policy dimension, and the notion of the bargaining set fits the situation of such free bargaining. One can use any coalition with any parties as a threat. If there is a single strong policy dimension, a coalition between the extreme right and the extreme left may be considered as scandalous and cannot be used as a threat. One cannot bargain freely with a single strong policy dimension. A proportional portfolio may be a good reference point where one cannot bargaining freely. If legislators cannot use their bargaining power freely, the result may be a "just" allocation of cabinet portfolios.

Japanese "parties" can be considered at different points along one ideological line. But, since there is almost no difference of ideology between L.D.P. factions,[13] they may also use pure bargaining to obtain cabinet posts.

Like Schofield and Laver (1985, 1987) I will test the hypotheses that the L.D.P. factions played a bargaining game for cabinet posts and the actual cabinet portfolio belonged to (1) the kernel of the game, (2) the bargaining set of the game.

Data

For the theoretical coordination with the kernel and bargaining set, we use the number of Lower House members of each faction as an independent variable. This is the same method as that used by Ishikawa (1984, p. 244) and Sato and Matsuzaki (1986, pp. 64, 65), who showed the proportionality of the portfolio of the cabinet to the size of the factions by making a table of them. We also add the members who temporarily left the factions to the factions they had belonged to, as Sato and Matsuzaki (1986, p. 242) have done. For the computation we consider independents as one faction, the "independents faction".

We use the number of the all ministerial positions allocated to each faction as the pay-off. We will compute the cases where factions try to get a simple majority of the Lower House and a stable majority in the Lower House. Since the total number in the Lower House was 511 before 1985 and 512 after 1986, a simple majority was 256 before 1985 and 257 after 1986. A simple majority is enough to get the prime minister and the cabinet, but not enough to ensure a smooth political process. With a stable majority in the Lower House, 271, one can get a majority on all committees in the Lower House and the political process becomes easy. We

THE LIBERAL DEMOCRATS AS A COALITION

also divide the cases where factions can use a coalition with the J.C.P. as a threat and where they cannot use it. In order to analyze the European coalition governments, Schofield and Laver (1985, 1987) assume all combinations of parties are possible. But I think coalition government with the J.C.P. is not plausible and want to check both possibilities.

Results

We examine the case of the 1980s when the coordinating structure clearly exists and the number of factions is reduced to five or six and membership of the factions was determined. The situation is suitable for the computation of the "kernel" or "bargaining set". But, still we need the help of a computer. Japan has too many parties and factions, compared with the Finnish cases cited before.

As Tables 38 to 40 show, the kernel does not explain outcomes well in all cases, just as it didn't work well with the European cases that were examined by Schofield and Laver (1985, 1987). The predicted number of the kernel clearly underestimates the big factions' power. It is the same problem as in the case presented by Schofield and Laver (1985, 1987). The kernel may not be a good predictor of the bargaining. As we saw in the introduction to this chapter, the kernel uses the notion of the amount of "regret" for its definition. This notion may be a little bit too subjective for getting the objective outcome of the game. It may also be a little bit arbitrary, especially if we compare it with the definition of the bargaining set.

The bargaining set explains most situations well. All actual portfolios are in a B1 bargaining set. A B1 bargaining set may be too big to give useful prediction, but B2 or B*, which is bigger than B2 but smaller than B1, works well, too. In the 1983 case, as Table 38 shows, a B* bargaining set predicts very well except for the overestimation of the "independents faction" and the underestimation of the New Liberal Club (N.L.C.). Since the N.L.C. was outside the L.D.P. during that time, though the members' origins were in the L.D.P., it may be natural that they had more bargaining power than L.D.P. factions. But in the 1986 case, as Table 39 shows, neither bargaining set succeeds in predicting the actualized portfolio, though the prediction is better than the prediction of proportional apportionment. However, if we deduct the posts assigned to the Upper House members and add the posts of the

36

Big Three of the L.D.P., as Ishikawa did (1984, p. 244, showing the proportionality of the portfolio of the cabinet to the size of the factions), the case of a stable majority with the J.C.P. predicts perfectly. As Table 40 shows, the 1990 case also may have the problem of the overestimation of the "independent faction".

It would be natural for the "independent faction" not to have enough power. It is not a perfect faction but an informal group. I consider it as a faction just for the computation. If we pay attention to the apportionment of the L.D.P.'s Big Three and the apportionment of a minister's position for the Upper House, I think the hypothesis that the actualized pay-off belongs to the bargaining set is supported by the result. We can take the view that the L.D.P. factions just played the bargaining game to obtain the positions, using the "threat" to form a coalition with opposition parties. We could consider the L.D.P. factions working like European parties under proportional representation systems.

Conclusion

As the foregoing analysis shows, the L.D.P. cabinet portfolio can be seen as the result of pure bargaining. Nakamura (1987) says that the difference between the Italian coalition of factions and the Japanese coalition of factions is that in Italy some factions within the original party break away from the party to form a new coalition with other parties. But this Italian style has also occurred in Japan. As the Japanese opposition parties became realistic contenders for power, the L.D.P. may have started to work with the same logic with which European coalition governments work. The mechanism of European style coalition government may have started almost fifteen years before the real or explicit coalition government that emerged in 1993.

In the election of the members of the Diet, the Japanese S.N.T.V. system worked as a semi-proportional system. It kept the number of seats in proportion to the number of votes.[14] As we saw in the introduction to this chapter, the Japanese S.N.T.V. system may give rise to strong factions. But they seem to have worked in much the same way as the European parties under the proportional representation system in forming coalition governments.

S.N.T.V. works similarly to the European proportional representation system, not only at the stage of transforming votes into seats but also at the stage of transforming seats into cabinet posts.

Since the S.N.T.V. makes the candidates more sensitive to the voters' wishes than under a proportional representation system with party-decided lists, it may be superior not only to the new Japanese election rule but also to the familiar system of proportional representation with a party-decided list of candidates.

4

THE ECONOMIC EFFECT
OF THE APPORTIONMENT
OF REPRESENTATIVES

Introduction

The study of the relationship between the polity and the economy
is very popular today. Much work has been done on public choice,
especially in the area of political economy. This includes work on
the political business cycle in the areas of macroeconomics,[1]
endogenous tariff formation,[2] the so-called theory of regulation,[3]
pressure groups[4] and the study of bureaucracy.[5]

In these studies, the distortion from many elements of the
political system such as the interval between elections, asset allocation,[6] the costs of organization and agenda control have been
analyzed. However, as far as I know, the economic inefficiency
caused by the misapportionment of representatives has not been
studied until now.

Though Japan and France may be the only major developed
countries with a remarkable malapportionment of their lower
houses,[7] there are several countries, such as the United States, that
have an upper house with highly unequal representation of votes
in different jurisdictions. It is also notable that Japan and France are
notorious for their protection of agriculture.

The main purpose of this chapter is to focus on the economic
distortion caused by the malapportionment of representatives and
to search for a way to eradicate such distortion. In the first section,
a criterion for triggering the political process (apportionment of
representatives) at the constitutional stage will be considered. In
the second and third sections an amendment that is a function of
population movements due to economic change will be studied. In
the third section we also introduce "sunk human capital" to
consider frictions caused by industrial reorganization.

An interesting conclusion in each scenario (at the constitutional stage, after the constitutional stage but without taking "sunk human capital" into consideration, and after the constitutional stage with "sunk human capital" taken into account) is that amendment of the apportionment of representatives is desirable even for the people who will end up with fewer representatives. Finally, this chapter closes with some concluding comments.

The story in the first section might be explained as follows. We will assume there are two areas in a country. Food is produced in the agricultural area by land and labor. Industrial goods are produced in the industrial area by capital and labor. To produce food and industrial goods efficiently and maximize the gross national product (G.N.P.), labor, which is assumed to be homogeneous, must be assigned between areas so that the value of the marginal product of labor (V.M.P.L.) in the agricultural area equals that in the industrial area. If the V.M.P.L. in the agricultural area is lower than in the industrial area, we can increase G.N.P. by moving some labor from the agricultural area to the industrial area. If the V.M.P.L. in the industrial area is lower than in the agricultural area, we can increase G.N.P. by moving some labor from the industrial area to the agricultural area. If the G.N.P. is maximized, the V.M.P.L. must be the same between two areas.

If both industries are competitive, the wage paid to a laborer is the same as the V.M.P.L. A profit-maximizing firm employs more laborers if the V.M.P.L. is higher than the wage, and fires some laborers if the V.M.P.L. is lower than the wage.

Laborers move to the area where they can get a higher wage. At equilibrium the wages in both areas are equal. So the V.M.P.L. in both areas is equal. This means that the country's G.N.P. is maximized by the movement of laborers in pursuit of higher wages. The wages are equal. There is no problem regarding the fairness of the distribution.

If we introduce government into this country, what will happen? What will the politicians do? English has the term "pork-barrel" and Japanese has a word, *Gaden-Intetsu*, which means the same thing. In most countries politicians try to attract as many financial resources as possible to their districts. Politicians present their achievements in terms of attracting government funds to the voters.

What will the voters or laborers do? Voters or laborers decide where to live or to work by considering not only their wages but also these benefits. They will choose the lower wage area if they can get bigger benefits to compensate for the lower wage. This means that the bigger benefits brought by politicians attract too many laborers and the V.M.P.L. in that area becomes lower than in the other area. This makes the production efficiency worse and the G.N.P. becomes smaller.

To keep the efficiency of production, *per capita* benefits must be equal between the areas. If the *per capita* benefits are the same between the areas, laborers move between the areas just for the higher wage. This makes the V.M.P.L. equal between two areas. It is a requirement for maximizing G.N.P.

The budget allocated to one area may increase as the number of its representatives increases. Therefore we should not give more representatives to a smaller population area (though this was done not only under the old Japanese election system but also under the new system). This unequal apportionment will give more of the budget to the small population area than to the big one. Clearly the *per capita* benefit in small population areas will be bigger than the *per capita* benefit in areas with a large population. This makes the G.N.P. smaller and the welfare of the people worse. If the budget for an area is proportional to the number of representatives, the number of the representatives must be proportional to the size of the population, to make the *per capita* benefits the same.

This criterion must be met in any situation if economic efficiency is to be achieved. The point is demonstrated in both the second and the third sections below. If the price of industrial goods rises and laborers move to the industrial area for a high wage, reapportionment of the representatives must be effected in order not to disturb the economic adjustment.

Let us examine a mathematical model to explain the same story in mathematics.

Taking apportionment into consideration at the constitutional stage

The pure economy

Let us set up the pure economy before the political process is introduced.

We will consider the two-sector (regions), two goods, three factors Jones–Neary type fixed factor model for a small country.

Here we have an agricultural sector which makes food (F) with land (T) and labor (L_F), and an industrial sector which makes industrial goods (M) with capital (K) and labor (L_M). (Labor will be assumed to move between the two sectors or regions freely.) Let us assume each laborer has the same amount of capital and land regardless of where he or she lives.[8] Then,

$$L_F + L_M = L \text{ (constant)} \tag{1}$$

Each sector's production function is[9]

$$F = F(L_F, T) \tag{2}$$
$$M = M(L_M, K) \tag{3}$$

We will define π as the industrial good's price in terms of the agricultural good's price, w_F as the wage in agriculture, and w_M as the wage in industry. In a competitive economy,

$$w_F = \frac{\partial F}{\partial L_F} \tag{4}$$

$$w_M = \pi \frac{\partial M}{\partial L_M} \tag{5}$$

The incomes from one unit of land (r) and capital (i) are

$$r = \frac{\partial F}{\partial T} \tag{6}$$

$$i = \pi \frac{\partial M}{\partial K} \tag{7}$$

Laborers in each sector have identical indirect utility functions with incomes of y_F and y_M,

$$V_F = V(\pi, y_F) \tag{8}$$
$$V_M = V(\pi, y_M) \tag{9}$$

The equilibrium obtained by moving to a different sector (region) will be the interior solution given by

$$V_F = V_M \tag{10}$$

which implies

$$y_F = y_M \tag{11}$$

Since each laborer has the same amount of capital and land, equilibrium in the economy is given by

$$w_F = w_M \tag{12}$$

This implies

$$\frac{\partial F}{\partial L_F} = \pi \frac{\partial M}{\partial L_M} \tag{13}$$

In other words, the value of the marginal product of each laborer is the same in both sectors. Let this L_F and L_M be denoted L_F^* and L_M^* respectively.

Introduction of the political process

Let us consider the introduction of a political process into this society. For simplicity, assume that the function of the political process is to divide a given benefit, G, among the areas. Each area has congressmen to represent it. Let us denote the number of each area's representatives as

$$R_F \; R_M(= R - R_F) \tag{14}$$

where R is the total number of representatives (constant). As in the general public choice model, we assume representatives do not maximize "social welfare" but work to benefit the area they represent so as to get re-elected. Let the total benefit for an area be a function of the number of representatives the area has.[10]

$$g_F = g(R_F) \tag{15}$$

$$g_M = g(R_M) \tag{16}$$

$$g(R_F) + g(R_M) = G \tag{17}$$

$$0 \leq g(R_F) \leq G \tag{18}$$

For simplicity we presume the benefit is a grant. The grant per laborer in each area will be[11]

$$s_F = \frac{g_F}{L_F} \tag{19}$$

and

$$s_M = \frac{g_M}{L_M} \tag{20}$$

We can consider the indirect utility function of the labor as

$$V_F = V(\pi, y_F + s_F) \tag{21}$$

$$V_M = V(\pi, y_M + s_M) \tag{22}$$

where y_x is earned income and $y_x + s_x$ is general income. The equilibrium will be an interior solution given by

$$V_F = V_M \tag{23}$$

that is,

$$y_F + s_F = y_M + s_M \tag{24}$$

Then we can rewrite (24) as

$$\frac{\partial F}{\partial L_F} + \frac{\dfrac{\partial F}{\partial T} T + \pi \dfrac{\partial M}{\partial K} K}{L} + \frac{g\,(R_F)}{L_F} = \pi \frac{\partial M}{\partial L_M} + \frac{\dfrac{\partial F}{\partial T} T + \pi \dfrac{\partial M}{\partial K} K}{L} + \frac{g\,(R_M)}{L_M} \tag{25}$$

Since in this model everyone's general income will be equal, the object at the constitutional stage will be to maximize

$$L_F \times [\frac{\partial F}{\partial L_F} + \frac{\dfrac{\partial F}{\partial T} T + \pi \dfrac{\partial M}{\partial K} K}{L} + \frac{g\,(R_F)}{L_F}] +$$

$$L_M \times [\pi \frac{\partial M}{\partial L_M} + \frac{\dfrac{\partial F}{\partial T} T + \pi \dfrac{\partial M}{\partial K} K}{L} + \frac{g\,(R_M)}{L_M}] =$$

$$\frac{\partial F}{\partial L_F} \times L_F + \frac{\partial F}{\partial T} \times T + \pi \frac{\partial M}{\partial L_M} \times L_M + \pi \frac{\partial M}{\partial K} K + g(R_F) + g(R_M) \tag{26}$$

with respect to L_F and L_M under the restriction that

$$L_F + L_M = L \tag{27}$$

Since we assume that the production function is homogeneous of degree 1, (26) is

$$F(L_F, T) + \pi M(L_M, K) + G \tag{28}$$

With T, K and G constant, maximizing (28) under the restriction that $L_F + L_M = L$ yields

$$\frac{\partial F}{\partial L_F} = \pi \frac{\partial M}{\partial L_M} \tag{29}$$

as a first order condition.

L_F and L_K that satisfy (29) are the equilibrium values of the pure economy, L_F^*, L_M^*. In other words we need to keep L_F and L_M when we introduce the political process. From the equilibrium equation in a world with political representation (25), we must introduce the political process while keeping

$$s_T = \frac{g(R_F)}{L_F^*} = \frac{g(R_M)}{L_M^*} + s_M \tag{30}$$

That is,

$$\frac{L_M^*}{L_F^*} = \frac{g(R_M)}{g(R_F)} \tag{31}$$

When the function $g(x) = kx$ (k constant) we need

$$\frac{L_M^*}{L_F^*} = \frac{kR_M}{kR_F} = \frac{R_M}{R_F} \tag{32}$$

Hence the criteria for apportionment in the constitutional stage are as follows:

1 When the local benefits obtained by representatives increase according to the number of representatives (i.e. $\partial g/\partial R_F > 0$, $\partial g/\partial R_M > 0$), as equation (31) implies, inverse apportionment is not desirable. That is to say, no region with a population smaller than that of another region should have more representatives than that other region.

2 When the local benefits obtained by representatives increase in proportion to the number of representatives (i.e. $g(x) = kx$, k constant), as equation (32) shows, the apportionment should be proportional to the population.

45

Taking apportionment into consideration after the constitutional stage

At the constitutional stage we may imagine that the apportionment of representatives is such that either benefits are equalized or the principle of "one man, one vote" is attained. After the constitutional stage, however, it may be difficult to adjust the apportionment of representatives.[12] In this section we will consider the effects of adjustment or the dynamics of the adjustment process itself. The conclusion of the analysis will then be used to analyze the case of Japan.

Let us call the time when the political process is introduced the first period, and the time following a shock to the economy the second period.[13]

Notation is the same as in the first section. For simplicity, let us assume that the benefits accruing to the population in each sector are equal to the number of representatives each sector has.

$$g_F = R_F \tag{33}$$

$$g_M = R_M \qquad (G = R) \tag{34}$$

The first period

From the first section we know that before the political process is introduced labor will be allocated efficiently through the process of voting with the feet because *per capita* land income and capital income are equal across sectors.

$$\frac{\partial F}{\partial L_F} = w_F = w_M = \pi \frac{\partial M}{\partial L_M} \tag{35}$$

Now let us introduce the political process designed in the first section. If it is "one man, one vote" the numbers of representatives satisfy (Let us put * on such L_F and L_M that satisfy.)

$$\frac{R_F}{L_F^*} = \frac{R_M}{L_M^*} \tag{36}$$

Let us put * on this R_F and R_M. Since *per capita* land income and *per capita* capital income are no different between constituencies, people voting with their feet means that an interior equilibrium is achieved and in the equilibrium (wage + benefit) is the same.

46

$$\frac{\partial F}{\partial L_F} + \frac{R_F^*}{L_F} = w_F + s_F = w_M + s_M = \pi \frac{\partial M}{\partial L_M} + \frac{R_M^*}{L_M} \tag{37}$$

Since there is no distortion by benefits, this implies

$$\frac{\partial F}{\partial L_F} = \pi \frac{\partial M}{\partial L_M} \tag{38}$$

Thus there is no distortion in production. That is, the optimal political process in the first section is introduced.

The second period

Let us assume that the international price of the industrial good rises $(\pi \to \pi [1 + p])$. By voting with their feet people in the agricultural sector in the first period will move in order to get the same general income as workers in the industrial sector.[14]

Let us redefine L_F and L_M as the first period equilibrium labor amount, R_F and R_M as the corresponding apportionment of representatives and s as the equal benefits they receive. If we define m as the moved labor in the second period, the level of general income when we do not adjust the apportionment of representatives will be

$$\frac{\frac{\partial F}{\partial L_F}(T, L_F - m) + \frac{L_F s}{L_F - m} + \frac{\partial F}{\partial T}(T, L_F - m) + \pi(1 + p)\frac{\partial M}{\partial K}(K, L_M + m)}{L} =$$

$$\frac{\pi(1 + p)\frac{\partial M}{\partial L_M}(K, L_M + m) + \frac{L_M s}{L_M + m} + \frac{\partial F}{\partial T}(T, L_F - m) + \pi(1 + p)\frac{\partial M}{\partial K}(K, L_M + m)}{L} \tag{39}$$

The level of general income when we adjust for the apportionment of representatives according to the population will be (let us define n as the movement of labor)

$$\frac{\partial F}{\partial L_F} (T, L_F - n) + s +$$

$$\frac{\frac{\partial F}{\partial T} (T, L_F - n) + \pi(1 + p) \frac{\partial M}{\partial K} (K, L_M + n)}{L} =$$

$$\pi(1 + p) \frac{\partial M}{\partial L_M} (K, L_M + n) + s +$$

$$\frac{\frac{\partial F}{\partial T} (T, L_F - n) + \pi(1 + p) \frac{\partial M}{\partial K} (K, L_M + n)}{L}$$

(40)

If we define the difference in general income as d

$$d > 0^{15}$$
(41)

It is obvious from the first section that apportionment should reflect the principle of "one man, one vote". In addition we have obtained a conclusion that suggests we should reapportion representatives when an unequal apportionment results from a shock to the economy.

Adjustment, however, may be a difficult process. First, under Japanese election law representatives themselves are responsible for reallocating seats between constituencies. The majority are elected from rural areas where the population is decreasing. They never want to reallocate seats or to see any committee on reallocation set up. Moreover, some argue that poor rural areas should not be robbed of representatives as well as population.

In the next section we will introduce the concept of "sunk human capital" and show how it affects the problem.

Taking apportionment into consideration after the constitutional stage with "sunk human capital"

We often see the word "friction" mentioned when reading about industrial reorganization or structural change in an economy. One element of this "friction" may be that the "sunk human capital" of an industry is being lost. In this section we introduce the concept of "sunk human capital" and reconsider the apportionment of representatives.

Let the amount of labor in efficiency units possessed by an individual be 1 in the first period and, in the second period, 1+c if he or she is in the same industry or 1 if he or she moves to another industry.

The first period

In the first period, each person has one efficiency unit of labor (denoted from here on with a hat, $\hat{}$). From the first section we know that before the political process is introduced labor will be allocated efficiently through the process of voting with the feet because *per capita* land and capital income are equal across sectors. That is,

$$\frac{\partial F}{\partial \hat{L}_F} = \hat{w}_F = w_F = w_M = \hat{w}_M = \pi \frac{\partial M}{\partial \hat{L}_M} \tag{42}$$

Now let us introduce the political process defined in the previous section. If it is "one man, one vote" the number of representatives will satisfy (we put * on the L_F and L_M which satisfy the pure economy equilibrium):

$$\frac{R_F}{L_F^*} = \frac{R_M}{L_M^*} \tag{43}$$

(Let us put * on such R_F and R_M.)

Since *per capita* land income and capital income are the same everywhere, voting with the feet means that an interior equilibrium will be attained, and in equilibrium general incomes (wages + benefits) will become identical.

$$\frac{\partial F}{\partial \hat{L}_F} + \frac{R_F^*}{L_F} = w_F + s_F = w_M + s_M = \pi \frac{\partial M}{\partial \hat{L}_M} + \frac{R_M^*}{L_M} \tag{44}$$

Since in the first period $L_F = \hat{L}_F$ and $L_M = \hat{L}_M$ and there is no distortion by the benefit, this equation implies

$$\frac{\partial F}{\partial \hat{L}_F} = \pi \frac{\partial M}{\partial \hat{L}_M} \tag{45}$$

There is no distortion of production efficiency. We have gotten the optimal political process as in the previous sections.

The second period

In this situation, in the second period, if the price rise is larger than human capital accumulation (in Cobb–Douglas terms $(1 + c)^{1+a-b} < (1 + p)^{16}$) the laborer will move.

Let us assume such a price rise has occurred. By voting with their feet some people who worked in the agricultural sector will move to get the same general income.

As in the previous section, let L_F and L_M be the pre-shock equilibrium populations and R_F and R_M the corresponding representatives. Let s be the amount of equal benefits each laborer receives.

If there is no reallocation of representatives, the level of general income of the people who worked in agriculture in the first period will be (let m be the amount of labor that moved):

$$
\frac{\partial F(T, (1 + c) (L_F - m))}{\partial L_F} (1 + c) + \frac{L_F s}{L_F - m} +
$$

$$
\frac{\dfrac{\partial F(T, (1 + c) (L_F - m))}{\partial T} T + \pi(1 + p) \dfrac{\partial M(K, L_M(1 + c) + m)}{\partial K} K}{L} =
$$

$$
\pi(1 + p) \frac{\partial M (K, L_M (1 + c) + m))}{\partial L_M} + \frac{L_M s}{L_M + m} +
$$

$$
\frac{\dfrac{\partial F(T, (1 + c) (L_F - m))}{\partial T} T + \pi(1 + p) \dfrac{\partial M(K, L_M(1 + c) + m)}{\partial K} K}{L} \tag{46}
$$

When we adjust the apportionment according to the population, the level of general income of the people who worked in the agricultural sector is (define n as the amount of labor that moved)

$$
\frac{\partial F(T, (1 + c) (L_F - n))}{\partial L_F} (1 + c) + s +
$$

$$
\frac{\dfrac{\partial F(T, (1 + c) (L_F - n))}{\partial T} T + \pi(1 + p) \dfrac{\partial M(K, L_M(1 + c) + n)}{\partial K} K}{L} =
$$

$$\pi(1 + p) \frac{\partial M(K, L_M(1 + c) + n))}{\partial L_M} + s +$$

$$\frac{\dfrac{\partial F(T, (1 + c) (L_F - n))}{\partial T} T + \pi(1 + p) \dfrac{\partial M(K, L_M(1 + c) + n)}{\partial K} K}{L} \tag{47}$$

If we define the difference in the general income as d,[17]

$$d > 0 \tag{48}$$

We might think that, if we adjusted the apportionment of the representatives, since the benefit would decrease, the general income in the agricultural area would decrease. But because of the fruits of economic efficiency this is not the result. Even though there is the "friction" associated with industrial reorganization, since the change in the economy was so great that some agricultural laborers willingly threw away their sunk human capital and moved to the industrial area, it is beneficial even for the people in the agricultural sector to adjust the apportionment of representatives and re-establish conditions of economic efficiency.

Concluding note

This chapter suggests that people who protect their benefits by political pressure may increase their own welfare level by unilaterally throwing away their excess political power (even if there are sunk human capital costs). This happens because the excess political power brought too much *per capita* benefit to the favored area and kept too many laborers in that area. It made the value of the marginal product or the wage in that area too low.

It may sound paradoxical and even odd to economists, who are used to seeing a trade-off between efficiency and equity, that seeking simple equity can raise efficiency. But this is reasonable when simple political equity is necessary to avoid distortion of the economy.

This chapter also suggests that promoting the movement of people from subsidized agricultural areas to cities will raise welfare levels. This is different from the "common sense view" in Japan. However, if we postulate that the low labor productivity of Japanese agriculture is attributable to overpopulation in rural areas and that congestion in city areas reflects the scarcity of social capital (i.e. infrastructure financed by government), it may not seem so strange.

To the best of my knowledge, no one has previously demonstrated that malapportionment can make even those in favored districts worse off. However, studies of the taxation of natural resources in federal systems have independently come up with the same general insight. See McLure (1983), Mieszkowski (1983) and Mieszkowski and Toder (1983). They examined the problem of natural resources distributed unequally among decentralized jurisdictions. Their logic is as follows. Suppose that natural resources are distributed unequally among decentralized jurisdictions (e.g. provinces or states) and that these resources are taxed at the jurisdiction (rather than the central) level. Then those states with high natural resource stocks can provide their residents with relatively attractive fiscal packages: high levels of services with relatively low taxes on residents (because of the revenues from taxes on their natural resources). This will tend to attract inefficiently large amounts of labor and capital into such jurisdictions until there is equalization of the level of utility among laborers across jurisdictions and until the net return to capital is equalized.

Our model works in a similar way. Both models describe processes that distort the economy and make it inefficient. But the origin of the problem is different. Our model analyzes a failure of pure politics. I hope the problem of unequal apportionment of representatives can be solved more easily, because we only need to insist on political justice: one man, one vote. The politicians from agricultural areas and their machine lose their privileges. They are the strongest group opposing reapportionment. But in the long run the wage in the agricultural areas as well as in the cities will be higher if the one man one vote principle is followed. Thus our result lends much credence to the ethical principle.

5

CONCLUDING REMARKS

We have examined the two distinguishing characteristics of the traditional Japanese election system: multi-member districts with S.N.T.V. and unequal apportionment.

The most commonly used election rules in the world are single-member districts with plurality and a proportional representation system with a party-decided list of candidates. Many Japanese politicians, journalists and even political scientists consider one or the other system ideal and criticize multi-member districts with S.N.T.V.

A presidential system like that of the United States, where each candidate for congress can freely choose his or her position just for his or her own victory, may result in a two-party system. But, as we have seen in Chapter 2, the prime ministership and single-member districts with a plurality system do not necessarily result in a two-party system. Without a guarantee of systematic political alternation between the two parties, multi-member districts with S.N.T.V. may be superior to single-member districts with a plurality system. Under the multi-party system, the multi-member districts with S.N.T.V. guarantee proportionality more than single-member districts with a plurality system would. From this point of view, multi-member districts with S.N.T.V. may be superior to one of the most common election rules, single-member districts with plurality.

As we have seen in Chapter 3, multi-member districts with S.N.T.V. make government formation similar to that in a proportional representation system. Since its proportionality at the electoral stage is almost similar to the proportional representation system, and the mechanism of its final stage, government formation, is almost the same, multi-member districts with S.N.T.V. may be better than the proportional representation system with a party-decided list of candidates. In the proportional representation system with a party-decided list of candidates it is most important for the person who wants to become a representative to have his or her name on the upper portion of the list of candidates. He or she tends to work for the party or the party leader and cares less about the voters. S.N.T.V. makes politicians more responsive to the voters. From this point of view, multi-member districts with S.N.T.V. may be superior to another common election rule, proportional representation with a party-decided list of candidates.

As we have seen in Chapter 4, amending the apportionment of representatives improves the welfare of the people. Unequal apportionment destroys both the fairness and the efficiency of the system. Many Japanese politicians, journalists and even political scientists approve of it, but I believe Japan needs to amend its apportionment from the viewpoints of both fairness and efficiency.

Despite the recent election reforms the Diet did not correct the unequal apportionment enough and decided to use an election system under which 300 of the members are chosen in single-member districts with plurality and the remaining 200 are chosen by the proportional representation system with a party-decided list of candidates in eleven districts. This change is the opposite of that suggested by our conclusion.

The consequences of the new election system have not been studied enough by politicians, journalists or even by political scientists or economists specializing in collective choice. This situation shows that the analytical level of Japanese work in collective choice and political science is not high enough. We need more theoretical studies.

Appendix 1

THE BARGAINING SET
AND THE KERNEL

Bargaining set

Let me introduce the definition of the bargaining set. For a simple majority game, winning coalitions are defined in the following way. Each player (in our context, factions and parties) $\{1, \ldots, n\}$ is assigned a weight $w(i)$ (in our context, the number of i faction's or i party's members per total representatives). The weight of coalition M is $w(M) - \Sigma_{i\in M}w(i)$. M is a winning coalition ($M\in W$), if $w(M) > \frac{1}{2}$ (for a simple majority game). The number, $v(M)$, is the value associated with coalition M; $v(M) > 0$ if $M\in W$ and $v(M) = 0$ if $M\notin W$. (In our context, $v(M)$ is the total seats in the cabinet (twenty-one) when M is a winning coalition ($M\in W$) and 0 when M is not a winning coalition ($M\notin W$).)

Definition 1 (Schofield 1987, p. 53)

For a general game, v, and coalition M, let $V(M)$ be the subset of $\mathbf{R}^n$ (n-dimension vector of the real number), defined as follows: $x\in V(M)$ if (1) $x_j = 0$ for all $j\notin M$, (2) $x_i \geq 0$ for all $i\in M$, (3) $\Sigma_{i\in M}x_i = v(M)$. (In our context, vector x shows the seats won by each faction and party.)

A pay-off configuration is a pair (x, M) where M is a coalition and $x = (x_1, \ldots, x_n)$ belongs to $V(M)$.

For the simplicity of notations and equations let us define T_{LJ} as the family of subsets which include subset L but do not intersect subset J.

Definition 2 (Schofield 1987, p. 53; 1982, p. 15)

$$T_{LJ} = \{A\subset N: L\subset A \text{ and } J\cap A = \varphi\}$$

55

Definition 3 (Schofield 1987, p. 53; 1982, p. 15)

Let (x, M) be a pay-off configuration and L, J two distinct subsets of the coalition M.

1 An objection by L against J with respect to (x, M) is a pay-off configuration (y, C), such that

    (a) $C \in T_{LJ}$
    (b) $y_i > x_i$ for all $i \in L$
    (c) $y_i \geq x_i$ for all $i \in C$

2 A counter-objection by J against L's objection (z, D) is a pay-off configuration, with

    (a) $D \in T_{JL}$
    (b) $z_j \geq x_i$ for all $j \in J$
    (c) $z_j \geq y_j$ for all $j \in D$

3 An objection (y, C) by L against J with respect to (x, M) is said to be justified if there is no counter-objection by J to (y, C). If L has a justified objection against J with respect to the pay-off configuration (x, M), then write $LP(x)J$.

Definition 4 (Schofield 1987, p. 54; 1982, p. 15; Ordeshook 1986, p. 400)

1 A pay-off configuration (x, M) is called B1-stable if to any objection by an individual i against an individual $j \in M/\{i\}$, there is a counter-objection by j. Let B1(M) be the set of B1-stable pay-off vector for M, and call B1(M) the B1 bargaining set for M. Thus

$$B1(M) = \left\{ x \in v(M) : (x, M) \text{ is B1--stable} \right\}$$

2 A pay-off configuration (x, M) is called B2-stable if to any objection by an individual i against any subgroup $J \subset M/\{i\}$, there is a counter-objection by J. Let B2(M) be the set of B2-stable pay-off vector for M, and call B2(M) the B2 bargaining set for M. Thus

$$B2(M) = \left\{ x \in v(M) : (x, M) \text{ is B2--stable} \right\}$$

Theorem 1 (Schofield 1987, p. 58; 1982, p. 16)

B2(M)⊂B1(M)

Proof: obvious.

Theorem 2 (Schofield 1987, p. 63; 1982, p. 16)

B1(M) is always non-empty.

Proof: see original.

Since B1(M) is too large and B2(M) is often empty, Schofield introduced B*(M), which always exists, and

B2(M)⊂B*(M)⊂B1(M)

Definition 5 (Schofield 1982, p. 18; 1987, p. 58)

1 Define iP*(x)j iff

(a) $x_j > 0$
(b)   For some K⊂M, K∈T$_{ij}$, iP(x)K and there is no
         L⊂M, L∈T$_{ij}$, such that L∩K ≠ φ, with jP(x)L.

2 B*(M) − { x∈v(M): iP*(x)j for no i, j in M }.

If iP(x)K for no K∋j, then not iP*(x)j, so B2(M)⊂B*(M).

If iP(x)j, then j cannot block this, so that iP*(x)j. Hence B*(M)⊂B1(M).

Kernel

Let me introduce the definition of the kernel.

Definition 6 (Schofield 1982, p. 17)

1 For a pay-off configuration (x, M) and coalition C, define the
   excess demand (or regret) of C over x to be

   $ex(C) = v(C) - \Sigma_{i \in C} x_i$

2 For L, J disjoint subsets in M define the surplus (or maximum
   excess demand or maximum regret) of L over J to be

   $S_{LJ}(x, M) = \max \left\{ ex(C): C \in T_{LJ} \right\}$

3 Say L outweighs J with respect to (x, M) iff

   (a) $S_{LJ}(x, M) > S_{JL}(x, M)$
   (b)   It is not the case that $x_j = 0$ $\forall j \in J$

4 A pay-off configuration (x, M) is called K1-stable if no individual i in M outweighs another $j \in M/\{i\}$. Write K1(M) for the K1-stable pay-off vector for M.

5 So K1(M) = $\{x \in v(M): (x, M)$ is a K1-stable pay-off configuration$\}$. Call K1 kernel for M. A pay-off configuration (x, M) is called K2-stable if no individual in M outweighs any group $J \subset M/\{i\}$. Call the K2-stable vectors the K2 kernel.

Theorem 3 (Schofield 1982, p. 17)

1 K2⊂K1
2 K1⊂B1
3 K2⊂B2

Proof: (1) obvious, (2) *see* Schofield (1987, p. 55), (3) *see* Schofield (1982, p. 17; 1978).

The K1 kernel is the kernel as defined in Owen (1982, p. 242), Shubik (1981, p. 304), Shubik (1982, p. 342), etc. Since the K2 kernel is usually empty (Schofield (1982, p. 18), I will mention only the K1 kernel as the kernel.

Appendix 2

TABLES

Table 1 Population and apportionment, 1889 election law (the first election, July 1st, 1890)

Prefecture	Population	Apportionment
Niigata	1681985	13
Tokyo	1628551	12
Hyogo	1541731	12
Aichi	1456294	11
Osaka	1324216	10
Hiroshima	1303457	10
Fukuoka	1224551	9
Chiba	1184062	9
Nagano	1128690	8
Shizuoka	1070841	8
Saitama	1069144	8
Okayama	1068086	8
Kumamoto	1052478	8
Ibaraki	1014354	8
Kagoshima	998153	7
Kanagawa	960069	7
Fukushima	934449	7
Yamaguchi	922497	7
Ehime	921708	7
Gifu	918456	7
Mie	918369	7
Kyoto	887031	7
Oita	788635	6
Nagasaki	762812	7
Miyagi	760291	5
Ishikawa	751605	6
Yamagata	750840	6
Toyama	745248	5
Gumma	722865	5
Tochigi	699121	5
Shimane	695782	6
Akita	690122	5
Tokushima	681863	5
Shiga	671788	5
Kagawa	668548	5
Iwate	667115	5
Wakayama	627332	5
Fukui	602342	4
Kochi	575852	4
Saga	560594	4
Aomori	538110	4
Nara	498871	4
Yamanashi	452781	3
Miyazaki	412729	3
Tottori	399060	3
Hokkaido		
Okinawa		
	39933478	300

Population data: December 31st, 1889 (The 12th Japan Imperial Almanac)
The ratio of *per capita* representatives between disadvantageous and advantageous prefectures = 1.40

Table 2 Population and apportionment, 1889 election law (the sixth election, August 10th, 1898)

Prefecture	Population	Apportionment
Tokyo	1948581	14
Niigata	1733629	13
Hyogo	1652366	12
Aichi	1592733	11
Osaka	1503771	10
Hiroshima	1405674	10
Fukuoka	1357777	9
Chiba	1245874	9
Nagano	1231859	8
Shizuoka	1175982	8
Saitama	1152823	8
Kumamoto	1122068	8
Ibaraki	1115269	8
Okayama	1108393	8
Kagoshima	1083745	7
Fukushima	1061013	7
Ehime	971955	7
Mie	967406	7
Yamaguchi	961065	7
Gifu	960713	7
Kyoto	957260	7
Kanagawa	870256	5
Nagasaki	845441	7
Miyagi	833113	5
Oita	819996	6
Yamagata	811039	6
Gumma	806277	5
Tochigi	798946	5
Akita	757041	5
Toyama	754799	5
Ishikawa	749775	6
Shimane	709065	6
Iwate	702750	5
Shiga	688343	5
Tokushima	676694	5
Kagawa	676681	5
Wakayama	656025	5
Fukui	612620	4
Kochi	609005	4
Aomori	600294	4
Saga	599679	4
Nara	524562	4
Yamanashi	492689	3
Miyazaki	455535	3
Tottori	412965	3
Hokkaido		
Okinawa		
	42773546	300

Population data: December 31st, 1897 (The 18th Japan Imperial Almanac)
The ratio of *per capita* representatives between disadvantageous and advantageous prefectures = 1.47

APPENDIX 2

Table 3 Population and apportionment, 1900 election law (the seventh election, August 10th, 1902)

Prefecture	Population	Apportionment
Tokyo	1978382	16
Hyogo	1716842	14
Niigata	1711744	14
Aichi	1607550	13
Osaka	1591105	13
Hiroshima	1461239	12
Fukuoka	1455111	14
Chiba	1260982	10
Nagano	1252999	10
Shizuoka	1202573	10
Kumamoto	1162659	9
Saitama	1160401	9
Ibaraki	1154255	10
Kagoshima	1121104	9
Okayama	1114746	9
Fukushima	1110548	9
Hokkaido	1003751	3
Ehime	991118	8
Kyoto	987717	8
Mie	978320	9
Yamaguchi	970039	8
Gifu	960946	8
Kanagawa	918905	8
Nagasaki	916764	8
Miyagi	857837	7
Yamagata	838175	8
Oita	834576	6
Tochigi	833162	7
Gumma	812424	8
Akita	789862	7
Toyama	746561	7
Ishikawa	722660	6
Iwate	720727	6
Shimane	708633	7
Kagawa	681658	7
Wakayama	673859	6
Tokushima	669643	6
Shiga	667149	6
Saga	628628	6
Aomori	628454	6
Kochi	619295	6
Fukui	607753	5
Nara	532076	5
Yamanashi	503605	5
Miyazaki	467840	4
Tottori	414241	4
Okinawa		
	44748618	376

Population data: December 31st, 1901 (The 22nd Japan Imperial Almanac)
The ratio of *per capita* representatives between disadvantageous and advantageous prefectures = 3.44 (incl. Hokkaido), 1.43 (excl. Hokkaido). In Hokkaido, representatives are only apportioned to city areas in this election, but population data include all, because the data of city areas are not available.

62

TABLES

Table 4 Population and apportionment, 1900 election law (the thirteenth election, April 20th, 1917)

Prefecture	Population	Apportionment
Tokyo	2890400	16
Osaka	2324700	13
Hyogo	2149200	14
Aichi	2076400	13
Niigata	1948400	14
Fukuoka	1920700	14
Hokkaido	1895100	6
Hiroshima	1681300	12
Shizuoka	1551900	10
Nagano	1509600	10
Kagoshima	1448000	9
Chiba	1401600	10
Saitama	1352000	9
Ibaraki	1336200	10
Kumamoto	1326600	9
Fukushima	1309200	9
Kyoto	1302900	8
Okayama	1271400	9
Kanagawa	1178200	8
Ehime	1136600	8
Gifu	1109300	8
Mie	1106900	9
Nagasaki	1103400	8
Yamaguchi	1091400	8
Tochigi	1039600	7
Gumma	1034300	8
Yamagata	987800	8
Miyagi	949700	7
Akita	949400	7
Oita	926800	6
Iwate	870200	6
Toyama	806200	7
Ishikawa	796200	6
Wakayama	794400	6
Aomori	777900	6
Kagawa	768800	7
Shimane	768600	7
Tokushima	740700	6
Kochi	717000	6
Saga	695800	6
Shiga	679600	6
Fukui	652600	5
Miyazaki	622700	4
Yamanashi	608300	5
Nara	600200	5
Okinawa	553300	2
Tottori	473500	4
	55235000	381

Population data: December 31st, 1916 (The 37th Japan Imperial Almanac)
The ratio of per capita representatives between disadvantageous and advantageous prefectures = 2.88 (incl. Hokkaido and Okinawa), 2.52 (excl. Hokkaido) 1.65 (excl. Hokkaido and Okinawa)

63

APPENDIX 2

Table 5 Population and apportionment, 1919 election law (the fourteenth election, May 10th, 1920)

Prefecture	Population	Apportionment
Tokyo	3457600	25
Osaka	2645500	20
Hyogo	2207500	18
Hokkaido	2137700	16
Aichi	2076800	17
Fukuoka	2029700	19
Niigata	1865600	17
Hiroshima	1629400	14
Shizuoka	1572600	13
Nagano	1542100	13
Kagoshima	1438100	11
Ibaraki	1375000	11
Chiba	1361100	11
Saitama	1357700	10
Fukushima	1356300	11
Kyoto	1336800	9
Kumamoto	1277400	10
Kanagawa	1268100	10
Okayama	1257400	10
Nagasaki	1182000	9
Ehime	1104600	9
Gifu	1094200	10
Mie	1088800	11
Yamaguchi	1069300	9
Tochigi	1067100	9
Gumma	1057300	9
Yamagata	975400	9
Akita	957300	8
Miyagi	937300	7
Oita	895300	8
Iwate	851400	7
Aomori	794400	7
Toyama	783400	7
Wakayama	782200	6
Ishikawa	768100	6
Tokushima	732800	6
Shimane	706600	7
Kochi	696300	6
Kagawa	693500	7
Shiga	675900	6
Saga	652400	6
Miyazaki	646600	5
Fukui	620000	6
Yamanashi	611600	5
Nara	582600	5
Okinawa	581500	5
Tottori	452900	4
	56253200	464

Population data: December 31st, 1919 (The 40th Japan Imperial Almanac)
The ratio of per capita representatives between disadvantageous and advantageous prefectures = 1.50

64

Table 6 Population and apportionment, 1919 election law (the fifteenth election, May 10th, 1924)

Prefecture	Population	Apportionment
Tokyo	3859400	25
Osaka	2926900	20
Hokkaido	2448900	16
Hyogo	2409100	18
Fukuoka	2261100	19
Aichi	2239200	17
Niigata	1825700	17
Shizuoka	1626700	13
Nagano	1602500	13
Hiroshima	1598400	14
Kagoshima	1452500	11
Fukushima	1416000	11
Ibaraki	1389200	11
Chiba	1382100	11
Saitama	1367700	10
Kyoto	1361400	9
Kanagawa	1353900	10
Kumamoto	1280000	10
Okayama	1235100	10
Nagasaki	1153900	9
Gifu	1113300	10
Gumma	1093700	9
Mie	1088200	11
Ehime	1085000	9
Tochigi	1084000	9
Yamaguchi	1076900	9
Miyagi	1022500	7
Yamagata	1002300	9
Akita	940100	8
Oita	895100	8
Iwate	880800	7
Aomori	784300	7
Wakayama	776000	6
Ishikawa	749600	6
Toyama	733100	7
Shimane	720600	7
Kagawa	693600	7
Tokushima	685100	6
Saga	683700	6
Kochi	681200	6
Miyazaki	676700	5
Shiga	658400	6
Fukui	600300	6
Yamanashi	592500	5
Nara	577000	5
Okinawa	569000	5
Tottori	466600	4
	58119300	464

Population data: October 1st, 1923 (Estimate by Statistics Bureau of Prime Minister's Office)
The ratio of *per capita* representatives between disadvantageous and advantageous prefectures = 1.56

Table 7 Population and apportionment, 1925 election law (the sixteenth election, February 20th, 1928)

Prefecture	Population	Apportionment
Tokyo	4897400	31
Osaka	3260000	21
Hokkaido	2612100	20
Hyogo	2531100	19
Aichi	2414600	17
Fukuoka	2386400	18
Niigata	1880700	15
Shizuoka	1723100	13
Nagano	1665900	13
Hiroshima	1648800	13
Kagoshima	1502300	12
Kanagawa	1495900	11
Fukushima	1476600	11
Kyoto	1462000	11
Ibaraki	1439700	11
Chiba	1426600	11
Saitama	1424900	11
Kumamoto	1326800	10
Okayama	1258700	10
Nagasaki	1204300	9
Gifu	1153800	9
Gumma	1152400	9
Ehime	1120100	9
Mie	1119600	9
Yamaguchi	1113100	9
Tochigi	1107100	9
Miyagi	1081500	8
Yamagata	1052400	8
Akita	947100	7
Oita	932800	7
Iwate	928600	7
Aomori	836500	6
Wakayama	803500	6
Toyama	762600	6
Ishikawa	753100	6
Shimane	727400	6
Kagawa	715600	6
Miyazaki	715300	5
Kochi	699000	6
Tokushima	696700	6
Saga	687400	6
Shiga	673500	5
Yamanashi	609100	5
Fukui	600400	5
Nara	585600	5
Okinawa	565400	5
Tottori	481900	4
	61659400	466

Population data: October 1st, 1927 (Estimate by Statistics Bureau of Prime Minister's Office) The ratio of per capita representatives between disadvantageous and advantageous prefectures = 1.40

TABLES

Table 8 Population and apportionment, 1925 election law (the twenty-first election, April 30th, 1942)

Prefecture	Population	Apportionment
Tokyo	7284300	31
Osaka	4661600	21
Hokkaido	3225600	20
Hyogo	3186800	19
Aichi	3124000	17
Fukuoka	3029700	18
Kanagawa	2191200	11
Niigata	2003300	15
Shizuoka	1976200	13
Hiroshima	1825500	13
Kyoto	1696100	11
Nagano	1651700	13
Ibaraki	1591100	11
Fukushima	1584100	11
Saitama	1580700	11
Chiba	1556800	11
Kagoshima	1547200	12
Nagasaki	1402100	9
Kumamoto	1321500	10
Okayama	1302300	10
Gumma	1276900	9
Yamaguchi	1269100	9
Miyagi	1240000	8
Gifu	1235900	9
Tochigi	1180800	9
Mie	1173000	9
Ehime	1158500	9
Yamagata	1085800	8
Iwate	1074900	7
Akita	1026400	7
Aomori	983800	6
Oita	949700	7
Wakayama	838400	6
Miyazaki	823900	5
Toyama	805400	6
Ishikawa	736600	6
Shimane	717800	6
Kagawa	708700	6
Tokushima	699100	6
Kochi	690700	6
Saga	689900	6
Shiga	686900	5
Fukui	623800	5
Yamanashi	623800	5
Nara	601300	5
Okinawa	566200	5
Tottori	471700	4
	71680200	466

Population data: October 1st, 1941 (Estimate by Statistics Bureau of Prime Minister's Office) The ratio of *per capita* representatives between disadvantageous and advantageous prefectures = 2.08

67

Table 9 Population and apportionment, 1945 election law (the twenty-second election, April 10th, 1946)

Prefecture	Population	Apportionment
Hokkaido	3518389	23
Tokyo	3488284	22
Aichi	2857851	18
Hyogo	2821892	18
Osaka	2800958	18
Fukuoka	2746855	18
Niigata	2389653	15
Shizuoka	2220358	14
Nagano	2121050	14
Saitama	2047261	13
Chiba	1966862	13
Fukushima	1957356	13
Ibaraki	1944344	13
Hiroshima	1885471	12
Kanagawa	1865667	12
Kyoto	1603796	10
Okayama	1564626	10
Kumamoto	1556490	10
Tochigi	1546355	10
Gumma	1546081	10
Kagoshima	1538466	11
Gifu	1518649	10
Miyagi	1462254	9
Mie	1394286	9
Ehime	1361484	9
Yamaguchi	1356491	9
Yamagata	1326350	9
Nagasaki	1318589	8
Iwate	1227789	8
Akita	1211871	8
Oita	1124513	7
Aomori	1083250	7
Toyama	953834	6
Wakayama	936006	6
Miyazaki	913687	6
Ishikawa	887510	6
Kagawa	863700	6
Shiga	860911	6
Shimane	860275	6
Yamanashi	839057	5
Tokushima	835763	5
Saga	830431	5
Nara	779685	5
Kochi	775578	5
Fukui	724856	5
Tottori	563220	4
Okinawa		
	71998104	466

Population data: November 1st, 1945 (Population Survey by Statistics Bureau of Prime Minister's Office)

The ratio of *per capita* representatives between disadvantageous and advantageous prefectures = 1.20

Table 10 Population and apportionment, 1947 election law (the twenty-third election, April 25th, 1947)

Prefecture	Population	Apportionment
Tokyo	4183072	27
Hokkaido	3488013	22
Osaka	2976140	19
Aichi	2919085	19
Fukuoka	2906644	19
Hyogo	2826192	18
Niigata	2326811	15
Shizuoka	2260059	14
Nagano	2028648	13
Saitama	2028553	13
Kanagawa	2019943	13
Chiba	2008568	13
Ibaraki	1940833	12
Fukushima	1918746	12
Hiroshima	1901430	12
Kumamoto	1631976	10
Kagoshima	1629760	10
Kyoto	1621998	10
Okayama	1538621	10
Gumma	1524635	10
Tochigi	1503619	10
Miyagi	1462100	9
Gifu	1444000	9
Nagasaki	1417977	9
Ehime	1380700	9
Yamaguchi	1375496	9
Mie	1371858	9
Yamagata	1294934	8
Iwate	1217154	8
Akita	1195813	8
Oita	1149501	7
Aomori	1089232	7
Miyazaki	957856	6
Wakayama	933231	6
Toyama	932669	6
Ishikawa	877197	6
Kagawa	872312	6
Saga	856692	5
Shimane	848995	5
Shiga	831306	5
Tokushima	829405	5
Kochi	797876	5
Yamanashi	796973	5
Nara	744381	5
Fukui	695703	4
Tottori	557429	4
Okinawa		
	73114136	466

Population data: April 26th, 1946 (Population Survey by Statistics Bureau of Prime Minister's Office)

The ratio of *per capita* representatives between disadvantageous and advantageous prefectures = 1.25

The ratio of *per capita* representatives between disadvantageous and advantageous districts = 1.51

Table 11 Population and apportionment, 1950 census and 1947 election law

Prefecture	Population	Apportionment
Tokyo	6277500	27
Hokkaido	4295567	22
Osaka	3857047	19
Fukuoka	3530169	19
Aichi	3390585	19
Hyogo	3309935	18
Kanagawa	2487665	13
Shizuoka	2471472	14
Niigata	2460997	15
Saitama	2146445	13
Chiba	2139037	13
Hiroshima	2081967	12
Fukushima	2062394	12
Nagano	2060831	13
Ibaraki	2039418	12
Kyoto	1832934	10
Kumamoto	1827582	10
Kagoshima	1804118	10
Miyagi	1663442	9
Okayama	1661099	10
Nagasaki	1645492	9
Gumma	1601380	10
Tochigi	1550462	10
Gifu	1544538	9
Yamaguchi	1540882	9
Ehime	1521878	9
Mie	1461197	9
Yamagata	1357347	8
Iwate	1346728	8
Akita	1309031	8
Aomori	1282867	7
Oita	1252999	7
Miyazaki	1091427	6
Toyama	1008790	6
Wakayama	982113	6
Ishikawa	957279	6
Kagawa	946022	6
Saga	945082	5
Shimane	912551	5
Tokushima	878511	5
Kochi	873874	5
Shiga	861180	5
Yamanashi	811369	5
Nara	763883	5
Fukui	752374	4
Tottori	600177	4
Okinawa	914937	
	84114574	466

Population data: October 1st, 1950 (Census)
The ratio of *per capita* representatives between disadvantageous and advantageous prefectures = 1.55
The ratio of *per capita* representatives between disadvantageous and advantageous districts = 2.17

TABLES

Table 12 Population and apportionment, 1955 census and 1947 election law

Prefecture	Population	Apportionment*
Tokyo	8037084	27
Hokkaido	4773087	22
Osaka	4618308	19
Fukuoka	3859764	19
Aichi	3769209	19
Hyogo	3620947	18
Kanagawa	2919497	13
Shizuoka	2650435	14
Niigata	2473492	15
Saitama	2262623	13
Chiba	2205060	13
Hiroshima	2149044	12
Fukushima	2095237	12
Ibaraki	2064037	12
Kagoshima	2044112	11
Nagano	2021292	13
Kyoto	1935161	10
Kumamoto	1895663	10
Nagasaki	1747596	9
Miyagi	1727065	9
Okayama	1689800	10
Gumma	1613549	10
Yamaguchi	1609839	9
Gifu	1583605	9
Tochigi	1547580	10
Ehime	1540628	9
Mie	1485582	9
Iwate	1427097	8
Aomori	1382523	7
Yamagata	1353649	8
Akita	1348871	8
Oita	1277199	7
Miyazaki	1139384	6
Toyama	1021121	6
Wakayama	1006819	6
Saga	973749	5
Ishikawa	966187	6
Kagawa	943823	6
Shimane	929066	5
Kochi	882683	5
Tokushima	878109	5
Shiga	853734	5
Yamanashi	807044	5
Nara	776861	5
Fukui	754055	4
Tottori	614259	4
Okinawa	801065	
	90076594	467

Population data: October 1st, 1955 (Census)
Apportionment: 1947 Election Law (added one seat of Amami to Kagoshima)
The ratio of per capita representatives between disadvantageous and advantageous prefectures = 1.94
The ratio of per capita representatives between disadvantageous and advantageous districts = 2.68

71

Table 13 Population and apportionment, 1960 census and 1947 election law

Prefecture	Population	Apportionment
Tokyo	9683802	27
Osaka	5504746	19
Hokkaido	5039206	22
Aichi	4206313	19
Fukuoka	4006679	19
Hyogo	3906487	18
Kanagawa	3443176	13
Shizuoka	2756271	14
Niigata	2442037	15
Saitama	2430871	13
Chiba	2306010	13
Hiroshima	2184043	12
Fukushima	2051137	12
Ibaraki	2047024	12
Kyoto	1993403	10
Nagano	1981506	13
Kagoshima	1963104	11
Kumamoto	1856192	10
Nagasaki	1760421	9
Miyagi	1743195	9
Okayama	1670454	10
Gifu	1638399	9
Yamaguchi	1602207	9
Gumma	1578476	10
Tochigi	1513624	10
Ehime	1500687	9
Mie	1485054	9
Iwate	1448517	8
Aomori	1426606	7
Akita	1335580	8
Yamagata	1320664	8
Oita	1239655	7
Miyazaki	1134590	6
Toyama	1032614	6
Wakayama	1002191	6
Ishikawa	973418	6
Saga	942874	5
Kagawa	918867	6
Shimane	888886	5
Kochi	854595	5
Tokushima	847274	5
Shiga	842695	5
Yamanashi	782062	5
Nara	781058	5
Fukui	752696	4
Tottori	599135	4
Okinawa	883122	
	94301623	467

Population data: October 1st, 1960 (Census)
Apportionment: 1947 Election Law (added one seat of Amami to Kagoshima)
The ratio of per capita representatives between disadvantageous and advantageous prefectures = 2.39
The ratio of per capita representatives between disadvantageous and advantageous districts = 3.21

Table 14 Population and apportionment, 1960 census and 1964 reapportionment

Prefecture	Population	Apportionment
Tokyo	9683802	39
Osaka	5504746	23
Hokkaido	5039206	22
Aichi	4206313	20
Fukuoka	4006679	19
Hyogo	3906487	19
Kanagawa	3443176	14
Shizuoka	2756271	14
Niigata	2442037	15
Saitama	2430871	13
Chiba	2306010	13
Hiroshima	2184043	12
Fukushima	2051137	12
Ibaraki	2047024	12
Kyoto	1993403	10
Nagano	1981506	13
Kagoshima	1963104	11
Kumamoto	1856192	10
Nagasaki	1760421	9
Miyagi	1743195	9
Okayama	1670454	10
Gifu	1638399	9
Yamaguchi	1602207	9
Gumma	1578476	10
Tochigi	1513624	10
Ehime	1500687	9
Mie	1485054	9
Iwate	1448517	8
Aomori	1426606	7
Akita	1335580	8
Yamagata	1320664	8
Oita	1239655	7
Miyazaki	1134590	6
Toyama	1032614	6
Wakayama	1002191	6
Ishikawa	973418	6
Saga	942874	5
Kagawa	918867	6
Shimane	888886	5
Kochi	854595	5
Tokushima	847274	5
Shiga	842695	5
Yamanashi	782062	5
Nara	781058	5
Fukui	752696	4
Tottori	599135	4
Okinawa	883122	
	94301623	486

Population data: October 1st, 1960 (Census)
The ratio of *per capita* representatives between disadvantageous and advantageous prefectures = 1.66
The ratio of *per capita* representatives between disadvantageous and advantageous districts = 2.19

Table 15 Population and apportionment, 1965 census and 1964 reapportionment

Prefecture	Population	Apportionment
Tokyo	10869240	39
Osaka	6657189	23
Hokkaido	5171800	22
Aichi	4798653	20
Kanagawa	4430743	14
Hyogo	4309944	19
Fukuoka	3964611	19
Saitama	3014983	13
Shizuoka	2912521	14
Chiba	2701770	13
Niigata	2398931	15
Hiroshima	2281146	12
Kyoto	2102808	10
Ibaraki	2056154	12
Fukushima	1983754	12
Nagano	1958007	13
Kagoshima	1853541	11
Kumamoto	1770736	10
Miyagi	1753126	9
Gifu	1700365	9
Okayama	1645135	10
Nagasaki	1641245	9
Gumma	1605584	10
Yamaguchi	1543573	9
Tochigi	1521656	10
Mie	1514467	9
Ehime	1446384	9
Aomori	1416591	7
Iwate	1411118	8
Akita	1279835	8
Yamagata	1263103	8
Oita	1187480	7
Miyazaki	1080692	6
Wakayama	1026975	6
Toyama	1025465	6
Ishikawa	980499	6
Kagawa	900845	6
Saga	871885	5
Shiga	853385	5
Nara	825965	5
Shimane	821620	5
Tokushima	815115	5
Kochi	812714	5
Yamanashi	763194	5
Fukui	750557	4
Tottori	579853	4
Okinawa	934176	
	99209133	486

Population data: October 1st, 1965 (Census)
The ratio of *per capita* representatives between disadvantageous and advantageous prefectures = 2.18
The ratio of *per capita* representatives between disadvantageous and advantageous districts = 3.23

Table 16 Population and apportionment, 1970 census and 1964 reapportionment

Prefecture	Population	Apportionment
Tokyo	11408070	39
Osaka	7620480	23
Kanagawa	5472247	14
Aichi	5386163	20
Hokkaido	5184287	22
Hyogo	4667928	19
Fukuoka	4027416	19
Saitama	3866472	13
Chiba	3366624	13
Shizuoka	3089895	14
Hiroshima	2436135	12
Niigata	2360982	15
Kyoto	2250087	10
Ibaraki	2143551	12
Nagano	1956917	13
Fukushima	1946077	12
Miyagi	1819223	9
Gifu	1758954	9
Kagoshima	1729150	11
Okayama	1707026	10
Kumamoto	1700229	10
Gumma	1658909	10
Tochigi	1580021	10
Nagasaki	1570245	9
Mie	1543083	9
Yamaguchi	1511448	9
Aomori	1427520	7
Ehime	1418124	9
Iwate	1371383	8
Akita	1241376	8
Yamagata	1225618	8
Oita	1155566	7
Miyazaki	1051105	6
Wakayama	1042736	6
Toyama	1029695	6
Ishikawa	1002420	6
Okinawa	945111	5
Nara	930160	5
Kagawa	907897	6
Shiga	889768	5
Saga	838468	5
Tokushima	791111	5
Kochi	786882	5
Shimane	773575	5
Yamanashi	762029	5
Fukui	744230	4
Tottori	568777	4
	104665170	491

Population data: October 1st, 1970 (Census)

Apportionment: 1964 reapportionment with five seats to Okinawa

The ratio of *per capita* representatives between disadvantageous and advantageous prefectures = 2.75

The ratio of *per capita* representatives between disadvantageous and advantageous districts = 4.83

Table 17 Population and apportionment, 1970 census and 1975
reapportionment

Prefecture	Population	Apportionment
Tokyo	11408070	43
Osaka	7620480	26
Kanagawa	5472247	19
Aichi	5386163	22
Hokkaido	5184287	22
Hyogo	4667928	20
Fukuoka	4027416	19
Saitama	3866472	15
Chiba	3366624	16
Shizuoka	3089895	14
Hiroshima	2436135	12
Niigata	2360982	15
Kyoto	2250087	10
Ibaraki	2143551	12
Nagano	1956917	13
Fukushima	1946077	12
Miyagi	1819223	9
Gifu	1758954	9
Kagoshima	1729150	11
Okayama	1707026	10
Kumamoto	1700229	10
Gumma	1658909	10
Tochigi	1580021	10
Nagasaki	1570245	9
Mie	1543083	9
Yamaguchi	1511448	9
Aomori	1427520	7
Ehime	1418124	9
Iwate	1371383	8
Akita	1241376	8
Yamagata	1225618	8
Oita	1155566	7
Miyazaki	1051105	6
Wakayama	1042736	6
Toyama	1029695	6
Ishikawa	1002420	6
Okinawa	945111	5
Nara	930160	5
Kagawa	907897	6
Shiga	889768	5
Saga	838468	5
Tokushima	791111	5
Kochi	786882	5
Shimane	773575	5
Yamanashi	762029	5
Fukui	744230	4
Tottori	568777	4
	104665170	511

Population data: October 1st, 1970 (Census)
The ratio of *per capita* representatives between disadvantageous and advantageous
prefectures = 2.06
The ratio of *per capita* representatives between disadvantageous and advantageous
districts = 2.92

Table 18 Population and apportionment, 1975 census and 1975 reapportionment

Prefecture	Population	Apportionment
Tokyo	11673550	43
Osaka	8278925	26
Kanagawa	6397748	19
Aichi	5923569	22
Hokkaido	5338206	22
Hyogo	4992140	20
Saitama	4821340	15
Fukuoka	4292963	19
Chiba	4149147	16
Shizuoka	3308799	14
Hiroshima	2646324	12
Kyoto	2424856	10
Niigata	2391938	15
Ibaraki	2342198	12
Nagano	2017564	13
Fukushima	1970616	12
Miyagi	1955267	9
Gifu	1867978	9
Okayama	1814305	10
Gumma	1756480	10
Kagoshima	1723902	11
Kumamoto	1715273	10
Tochigi	1698003	10
Mie	1626002	9
Nagasaki	1571912	9
Yamaguchi	1555218	9
Aomori	1468646	7
Ehime	1465215	9
Iwate	1385563	8
Akita	1232481	8
Yamagata	1220302	8
Oita	1190314	7
Miyazaki	1085055	6
Nara	1077491	5
Wakayama	1072118	6
Toyama	1070791	6
Ishikawa	1069872	6
Okinawa	1042572	5
Shiga	985621	5
Kagawa	961292	6
Saga	837674	5
Kochi	808397	5
Tokushima	805166	5
Yamanashi	783050	5
Fukui	773599	4
Shimane	768886	5
Tottori	581311	4
	111939639	511

Population data: October 1st, 1975 (Census)
The ratio of per capita representatives between disadvantageous and advantageous prefectures = 2.32
The ratio of per capita representatives between disadvantageous and advantageous districts = 3.72

APPENDIX 2

Table 19 Population and apportionment, 1980 census and 1975 reapportionment

Prefecture	Population	Apportionment
Tokyo	11618280	43
Osaka	8473446	26
Kanagawa	6924348	19
Aichi	6221638	22
Hokkaido	5575989	22
Saitama	5420480	15
Hyogo	5144892	20
Chiba	4735424	16
Fukuoka	4553461	19
Shizuoka	3446804	14
Hiroshima	2739161	12
Ibaraki	2558007	12
Kyoto	2527330	10
Niigata	2451357	15
Nagano	2083934	13
Miyagi	2082320	9
Fukushima	2035272	12
Gifu	1960107	9
Okayama	1871023	10
Gumma	1848562	10
Tochigi	1792201	10
Kumamoto	1790327	10
Kagoshima	1784623	11
Mie	1686936	9
Nagasaki	1590564	9
Yamaguchi	1587079	9
Aomori	1523907	7
Ehime	1506637	9
Iwate	1421927	8
Akita	1256745	8
Yamagata	1251917	8
Oita	1228913	7
Nara	1209365	5
Miyazaki	1151587	6
Ishikawa	1119304	6
Okinawa	1106559	5
Toyama	1103459	6
Wakayama	1087012	6
Shiga	1079898	5
Kagawa	999864	6
Saga	865574	5
Kochi	831275	5
Tokushima	825261	5
Yamanashi	804256	5
Fukui	794354	4
Shimane	784795	5
Tottori	604221	4
	117060395	511

Population data: October 1st, 1980 (Census)
The ratio of per capita representatives between disadvantageous and advantageous prefectures = 2.41
The ratio of per capita representatives between disadvantageous and advantageous districts = 4.54

78

Table 20 Population and apportionment, 1985 census and 1975 reapportionment

Prefecture	Population	Apportionment
Tokyo	11829360	43
Osaka	8668095	26
Kanagawa	7431974	19
Aichi	6455172	22
Saitama	5863678	15
Hokkaido	5679439	22
Hyogo	5278050	20
Chiba	5148163	16
Fukuoka	4719259	19
Shizuoka	3574692	14
Hiroshima	2819200	12
Ibaraki	2725005	12
Kyoto	2586574	10
Niigata	2478470	15
Miyagi	2176295	9
Nagano	2136927	13
Fukushima	2080304	12
Gifu	2028536	9
Gumma	1921259	10
Okayama	1916906	10
Tochigi	1866066	10
Kumamoto	1837747	10
Kagoshima	1819270	11
Mie	1747311	9
Yamaguchi	1601627	9
Nagasaki	1593968	9
Ehime	1529983	9
Aomori	1524448	7
Iwate	1433611	8
Nara	1304866	5
Yamagata	1261662	8
Akita	1254032	8
Oita	1250214	7
Okinawa	1179097	5
Miyazaki	1175543	6
Shiga	1155844	5
Ishikawa	1152325	6
Toyama	1118369	6
Wakayama	1087206	6
Kagawa	1022569	6
Saga	880013	5
Kochi	839784	5
Tokushima	834889	5
Yamanashi	832832	5
Fukui	817633	4
Shimane	794629	5
Tottori	616024	4
	121048920	511

Population data: October 1st, 1985 (Census)
The ratio of *per capita* representatives between disadvantageous and advantageous prefectures = 2.54
The ratio of *per capita* representatives between disadvantageous and advantageous districts = 5.12

Table 21 Population and apportionment, 1985 census and 1986 reapportionment

Prefecture	Population	Apportionment
Tokyo	11829360	44
Osaka	8668095	27
Kanagawa	7431974	20
Aichi	6455172	22
Saitama	5863678	17
Hokkaido	5679439	23
Hyogo	5278050	19
Chiba	5148163	18
Fukuoka	4719259	19
Shizuoka	3574692	14
Hiroshima	2819200	12
Ibaraki	2725005	12
Kyoto	2586574	10
Niigata	2478470	13
Miyagi	2176295	9
Nagano	2136927	13
Fukushima	2080304	12
Gifu	2028536	9
Gumma	1921259	10
Okayama	1916906	10
Tochigi	1866066	10
Kumamoto	1837747	10
Kagoshima	1819270	10
Mie	1747311	9
Yamaguchi	1601627	9
Nagasaki	1593968	9
Ehime	1529983	9
Aomori	1524448	7
Iwate	1433611	8
Nara	1304866	5
Yamagata	1261662	7
Akita	1254032	7
Oita	1250214	7
Okinawa	1179097	5
Miyazaki	1175543	6
Shiga	1155844	5
Ishikawa	1152325	5
Toyama	1118369	6
Wakayama	1087206	6
Kagawa	1022569	6
Saga	880013	5
Kochi	839784	5
Tokushima	834889	5
Yamanashi	832832	5
Fukui	817633	4
Shimane	794629	5
Tottori	616024	4
	121048920	512

Population data: October 1st, 1985 (Census)
The ratio of per capita representatives between disadvantageous and advantageous prefectures = 2.41
The ratio of per capita representatives between disadvantageous and advantageous districts = 2.99

Table 22 Population and apportionment, 1990 census and 1986
reapportionment

Prefecture	Population	Apportionment
Tokyo	11855563	44
Osaka	8734516	27
Kanagawa	7980391	20
Aichi	6690603	22
Saitama	6405319	17
Hokkaido	5643647	23
Chiba	5555429	18
Hyogo	5405040	19
Fukuoka	4811050	19
Shizuoka	3670840	14
Hiroshima	2849847	12
Ibaraki	2845382	12
Kyoto	2602460	10
Niigata	2474583	13
Miyagi	2248558	9
Nagano	2156627	13
Fukushima	2104058	12
Gifu	2066569	9
Gumma	1966265	10
Tochigi	1935168	10
Okayama	1925877	10
Kumamoto	1840326	10
Kagoshima	1797824	10
Mie	1792514	9
Yamaguchi	1572616	9
Nagasaki	1562959	9
Ehime	1515025	9
Aomori	1482873	7
Iwate	1416928	8
Nara	1375481	5
Yamagata	1258390	7
Oita	1236942	7
Akita	1227478	7
Shiga	1222411	5
Okinawa	1222398	5
Miyazaki	1168907	6
Ishikawa	1164628	5
Toyama	1120161	6
Wakayama	1074325	6
Kagawa	1023412	6
Saga	877851	5
Yamanashi	852966	5
Tokushima	831598	5
Kochi	825034	5
Fukui	823585	4
Shimane	781021	5
Tottori	615722	4
	123611167	512

Population data: October 1st, 1990 (Census)
The ratio of *per capita* representatives between disadvantageous and advantageous prefectures = 2.59
The ratio of *per capita* representatives between disadvantageous and advantageous districts = 3.38

Table 23 Population and apportionment (current situation), 1990 census and 1992 reapportionment (current situation)

Prefecture	Population	Apportionment
Tokyo	11855563	43
Osaka	8734516	28
Kanagawa	7980391	22
Aichi	6690603	22
Saitama	6405319	20
Hokkaido	5643647	23
Chiba	5555429	19
Hyogo	5405040	19
Fukuoka	4811050	20
Shizuoka	3670840	14
Hiroshima	2849847	13
Ibaraki	2845382	12
Kyoto	2602460	10
Niigata	2474583	13
Miyagi	2248558	8
Nagano	2156627	12
Fukushima	2104058	12
Gifu	2066569	9
Gumma	1966265	10
Tochigi	1935168	10
Okayama	1925877	10
Kumamoto	1840326	9
Kagoshima	1797824	9
Mie	1792514	8
Yamaguchi	1572616	9
Nagasaki	1562959	9
Ehime	1515025	9
Aomori	1482873	7
Iwate	1416928	7
Nara	1375481	5
Yamagata	1258390	7
Oita	1236942	6
Akita	1227478	7
Shiga	1222411	5
Okinawa	1222398	5
Miyazaki	1168907	5
Ishikawa	1164628	5
Toyama	1120161	6
Wakayama	1074325	5
Kagawa	1023412	6
Saga	877851	5
Yamanashi	852966	5
Tokushima	831598	5
Kochi	825034	5
Fukui	823585	4
Shimane	781021	5
Tottori	615722	4
	123611167	511

Population data: October 1st, 1990 (Census)
The ratio of *per capita* representatives between disadvantageous and advantageous prefectures = 2.36
The ratio of *per capita* representatives between disadvantageous and advantageous districts = 2.77

Table 24 New apportionment for prefectures and ideal apportionments
(1994 election law and October 1st, 1990 census)

Prefecture	Quota	New	Ham	Adam	Dean	Hill	Web	Jef
Tokyo	28.77	25	29	27	29	29	29	30
Osaka	21.20	19	21	20	21	21	21	22
Kanagawa	19.37	17	19	18	19	19	19	20
Aichi	16.24	15	16	16	16	16	16	17
Saitama	15.55	14	16	15	15	15	16	16
Hokkaido	13.70	13	14	13	14	14	14	14
Chiba	13.48	12	13	13	13	13	14	14
Hyogo	13.12	12	13	13	13	13	13	14
Fukuoka	11.68	11	12	11	12	12	12	12
Shizuoka	8.91	9	9	9	9	9	9	9
Hiroshima	6.92	7	7	7	7	7	7	7
Ibaraki	6.91	7	7	7	7	7	7	7
Kyoto	6.32	6	6	6	6	6	6	6
Niigata	6.01	6	6	6	6	6	6	6
Miyagi	5.46	6	5	6	5	5	5	5
Nagano	5.23	5	5	5	5	5	5	5
Fukushima	5.11	5	5	5	5	5	5	5
Gifu	5.02	5	5	5	5	5	5	5
Gumma	4.77	5	5	5	5	5	5	5
Tochigi	4.70	5	5	5	5	5	5	5
Okayama	4.67	5	5	5	5	5	5	4
Kumamoto	4.47	5	4	5	4	4	4	4
Kagoshima	4.36	5	4	5	4	4	4	4
Mie	4.35	5	4	5	4	4	4	4
Yamaguchi	3.82	4	4	4	4	4	4	4
Nagasaki	3.79	4	4	4	4	4	4	4
Ehime	3.68	4	4	4	4	4	4	3
Aomori	3.60	4	4	4	4	4	4	3
Iwate	3.44	4	3	4	3	3	3	3
Nara	3.34	4	3	4	3	3	3	3
Yamagata	3.05	4	3	3	3	3	3	3
Oita	3.00	4	3	3	3	3	3	3
Akita	2.98	3	3	3	3	3	3	3
Shiga	2.97	3	3	3	3	3	3	3
Okinawa	2.97	3	3	3	3	3	3	3
Miyazaki	2.84	3	3	3	3	3	3	3
Ishikawa	2.83	3	3	3	3	3	3	3
Toyama	2.72	3	3	3	3	3	3	2
Wakayama	2.61	3	3	3	3	3	3	2
Kagawa	2.48	3	2	3	3	3	2	2
Saga	2.13	3	2	2	2	2	2	2
Yamanashi	2.07	3	2	2	2	2	2	2
Tokushima	2.02	3	2	2	2	2	2	2
Kochi	2.00	3	2	2	2	2	2	2
Fukui	2.00	3	2	2	2	2	2	2
Shimane	1.90	3	2	2	2	2	2	2
Tottori	1.49	2	2	2	2	2	1	1
	300	300	300	300	300	300	300	300

Ham: Hamilton's Method (Method of Largest Remainder)
Adam: Adam's Method
Dean: Dean's Method
Hill: Hill's Method (Method of U.S. Lower House)
Web: Webster's Method (Method of Sainte Lague)
Jef: Jefferson's Method (Method of d'Hondt) (See Balinski and Young 1982)

Table *25* New apportionment of the Lower House for the areas

Area	Population	P.R. part	Districts	Total
Kinki	20414233	33		80
Osaka	8734516		19	
Hyogo	5405040		12	
Kyoto	2602460		6	
Nara	1375481		4	
Shiga	1222411		3	
Wakayama	1074325		3	
Kyushu	14518257	23		61
Fukuoka	4811050		11	
Kumamoto	1840326		5	
Kagoshima	1797824		5	
Nagasaki	1562959		4	
Oita	1236942		4	
Okinawa	1222398		3	
Miyazaki	1168907		3	
Saga	877851		3	
Minami-Kanto	14388786	23		55
Kanagawa	7980391		17	
Chiba	5555429		12	
Yamanashi	852966		3	
Tokai	14220526	23		57
Aichi	6690603		15	
Shizuoka	3670840		9	
Gifu	2066569		5	
Mie	1792514		5	
Kita-Kanto	13152134	21		52
Saitama	6405319		14	
Ibaraki	2845382		7	
Gumma	1966265		5	
Tochigi	1935168		5	
Tokyo	11855563	19		44
Tokyo	11855563		25	
Tohoku	9738285	16		42
Miyagi	2248558		6	
Fukushima	2104058		5	
Aomori	1482873		4	
Iwate	1416928		4	
Yamagata	1258390		4	
Akita	1227478		3	
Chugoku	7745083	13		34
Hiroshima	2849847		7	
Okayama	1925877		5	
Yamaguchi	1572616		4	
Shimane	781021		3	
Tottori	615722		2	

Table 25 continued

Hokushinetsu	7739584	13		33
Niigata	2474583		6	
Nagano	2156627		5	
Ishikawa	1164628		3	
Toyama	1120161		3	
Fukui	823585		3	
Hokkaido	5643647	9		22
Hokkaido	5643647		13	
Shikoku	4195069	7		20
Ehime	1515025		4	
Kagawa	1023412		3	
Tokushima	831598		3	
Kochi	825034		3	
Total	123611167	200	300	500

Table 26 Examples of overnomination and unequal vote distribution in the Japanese Lower House election, 1993

A Unequal vote distribution (L.D.P.)
   Yamagata, first district, four seats

Michihiko Kano	(L.D.P.)	103,559	elected
Tetsuo Kondo	(L.D.P.)	81,731	elected
Toshiaki Endo	(Indep.)	75,477	elected
Noboru Endo	(J.S.P.)	70,606	elected
Takehiko Endo	(L.D.P.)	69,437	
Tatsuo Inoue	(J.C.P.)	12,363	

B Overnomination (J.S.P.)
   Hokkaido, fifth district, five seats

Shoichi Nakagawa	(L.D.P.)	110,832	elected
Naoto Kitamura	(J.R.P.)	107,295	elected
Tsutomu Takebe	(L.D.P.)	87,944	elected
Muneo Suzuki	(L.D.P.)	85,201	elected
Tetsuo Nagai	(Indep.)	71,422	elected
Toshiharu Okada	(J.S.P.)	68,236	
Ryuji Ikemoto	(J.S.P.)	61,328	
Terumi Muraguchi	(J.C.P.)	26,136	
Tokuhei Akibe	(Indep.)	5,686	

Table 27 Inquiry of Japan Election Studies Association (%)

The biggest ratio of the *per capita* representatives between constituencies	
Must be less than 1:2	69.8
Is acceptable if it is around 1:3	10.4
Cannot be decided just by the number	17.0
(Other)	2.8

The situation where a less populated constituency has more representatives	
Is acceptable if the ratio is adjusted	36.8
Must not be there	57.5
(Other)	5.7

Table 28 Solving the game of Chapter 2, case 1
($\#\alpha > \#\beta$, $\#\gamma$; $\#\alpha > \#\beta + \#\gamma$; $\#\alpha + \#\beta\alpha > \#\beta\gamma + \#\gamma$; $\#\alpha + \#\beta > \#\gamma$)
A = Biggest = Condorcet winner = A (A = Dominant)

A	B	C	Winner	
Run	Run	Run	A	Nash Trembling hand
Run	Run	Exit *	A	Nash
Run	Exit *	Run	A	Nash
Run	Exit *	Exit *	A	Nash
Exit X	Run	Run	B	
Exit X	Run	Exit	B	
Exit X	Exit X	Run	C	
Exit X	Exit X	Exit X	X	

Since the strategies with "X" are not optimal strategies for the candidate, given other candidates' strategies, the sets of the strategies without "X" are Nash equilibria in pure strategy. The Nash equilibrium strategies with "*" are not optimal strategies for the candidate in the perturbed games. In this model it can be proved that the set of strategies without "*" is the (unique) trembling hand perfect equilibrium.

Table 29 Solving the game of Chapter 2, case 2
($\#\alpha > \#\beta$, $\#\gamma$; $\#\alpha < \#\beta + \#\gamma$; $\#\alpha + \#\beta\alpha > \#\beta\gamma + \#\gamma$; $\#\alpha + \#\beta > \#\gamma$)
A = Biggest ≠ Condorcet winner = B

A	B	C	Winner	
Run	Run	Run X	A	
Run	Run	Exit	B	Nash Trembling hand
Run	Exit *	Run	A	Nash
Run	Exit X	Exit	A	
Exit X	Run	Run	B	
Exit *	Run	Exit	B	Nash
Exit X	Exit X	Run	C	
Exit X	Exit X	Exit X	X	

Table 30 Solving the game of Chapter 2, case 3-1 (B prefers A to C)
(#α > #β, #γ; #α < #β + #γ; #α < #β + #γ; #α + #βα < #βγ + #γ; #α + #β > #γ)
A = Biggest ≠ Condorcet winner = B

A	B	C	Winner
Run	Run	Run X	A
Run	Run	Exit	B Nash Trembling hand
Run	Exit X	Run	C
Run	Exit X	Exit X	A
Exit X	Run	Run	B
Exit *	Run	Exit	B Nash
Exit	Exit X	Run	C
Exit X	Exit X	Exit X	X

Table 31 Solving the game of Chapter 2, case 3-2 (B prefers C to A)
(#α > #β, #γ; #α < #β + #γ; #α + #βα < #βγ + #γ; #α + #β > #γ)
A = Biggest ≠ Condorcet winner = B

A	B	C	Winner
Run	Run X	Run X	A Chicken
Run	Run	Exit	B Nash Trembling hand
Run	Exit	Run	C Nash Trembling hand
Run	Exit X	Exit X	A
Exit X	Run	Run	B
Exit *	Run	Exit	B Nash
Exit	Exit X	Run	C
Exit X	Exit X	Exit X	X

Table 32 Solving the game of Chapter 2, case 4
(#β > #α, #γ; #α < #β + #γ; #α + #βα > #βγ + #γ; #α + #β > #γ)
B = Biggest = Condorcet winner = B

A	B	C	Winner
Run	Run	Run	B Nash Trembling hand
Run	Run	Exit *	B Nash
Run	Exit X	Run	A
Run	Exit X	Exit	A
Exit *	Run	Run	B Nash
Exit *	Run	Exit *	B Nash
Exit X	Exit X	Run	C
Exit X	Exit X	Exit X	X

87

Table 33 Solving the game of Chapter 2, case 5
(#β > #α, #γ; #α < #β + #γ; #α + #βα < #βγ + #γ; #α + #β > #γ)
B = Biggest = Condorcet winner = B

A	B	C	Winner	
Run	Run	Run	B	Nash Trembling hand
Run	Run	Exit *	B	Nash
Run	Exit X	Run	C	
Run	Exit X	Exit X	A	
Exit *	Run	Run	B	Nash
Exit *	Run	Exit *	B	Nash
Exit	Exit X	Run	C	
Exit X	Exit X	Exit X	X	

Table 34 Solving the game of Chapter 2, case 6-1 (B prefers A to C)
(#γ > #α, #β; #α < #β + #γ; #α + #βα > #βγ + #γ; #α + #β > #γ)
C = Biggest ≠ Condorcet winner = B

A	B	C	Winner	
Run X	Run X	Run	C	Chicken
Run	Run	Exit X	B	
Run	Exit	Run	A	Nash Trembling hand
Run	Exit X	Exit	A	
Exit	Run	Run	B	Nash Trembling hand
Exit	Run	Exit *	B	Nash
Exit X	Exit X	Run	C	
Exit X	Exit X	Exit X	X	

Table 35 Solving the game of Chapter 2, case 6-2 (B prefers C to A)
(#γ > #α, #β; #α < #β + #γ; #α + #βα > #βγ + #γ; #α + #β > #γ)
C = Biggest ≠ Condorcet winner = B

A	B	C	Winner	
Run X	Run	Run	C	
Run	Run	Exit X	B	
Run	Exit X	Run	A	
Run	Exit X	Exit	A	
Exit	Run	Run	B	Nash Trembling hand
Exit	Run	Exit *	B	Nash
Exit X	Exit X	Run	C	
Exit X	Exit X	Exit X	X	

Table 36 Solving the game of Chapter 2, case 7
($\#\gamma > \#\alpha$, $\#\beta$; $\#\alpha < \#\beta + \#\gamma$; $\#\alpha + \#\beta\alpha < \#\beta\gamma + \#\gamma$; $\#\alpha + \#\beta > \#\gamma$)
C = Biggest ≠ Condorcet winner = B

A	B	C	Winner	
Run X	Run	Run	C	
Run	Run	Exit X	B	
Run	Exit *	Run	C	Nash
Run	Exit X	Exit X	A	
Exit	Run	Run	B	Nash Trembling hand
Exit	Run	Exit *	B	Nash
Exit	Exit X	Run	C	
Exit X	Exit X	Exit X	X	

Table 37 Solving the game of Chapter 2, case 8
($\#\gamma > \#\alpha$, $\#\beta$; $\#\alpha < \#\beta + \#\gamma$; $\#\alpha + \#\beta\alpha < \#\beta\gamma + \#\gamma$; $\#\alpha + \#\beta < \#\gamma$)
C = Biggest = Condorcet winner = C (C=Dominant)

A	B	C	Winner	
Run	Run	Run	C	Nash Trembling hand
Run	Run	Exit X	B	
Run	Exit *	Run	C	Nash
Run	Exit X	Exit X	A	
Exit *	Run	Run	C	Nash
Exit	Run	Exit X	B	
Exit *	Exit *	Run	C	Nash
Exit X	Exit X	Exit X	X	

Table 38 After the thirty-seventh general election, 1983

	Tanaka	Suzuki	Nakasone	Fukuda	Komoto	Indep.	N.L.C.	Nakagawa
					Nakasone second cabinet, December 27tb			
Lower House	63	50	50	42	28	22	8	6
Inside( )	Finance	Justice	Prime	Foreign	Labor		Home.Af.	
Assigned to	Health	Const.	Trade	Educat.	Eco.Pl.			
Upper House	Agri.	Defence	Secret.	Transp.				
	Posts	(Sci.)	(Hokkai)	Gen.Mg.				
	Admin.							
	(Enviro.)							
Pay-off	6	4	4	4	2	0	1	0
Big 3 of L.D.P	Ex.Coun.	Sec.Gen.		PARC				
Proportional	4.92	3.90	3.90	3.28	2.19	1.72	0.62	0.47
Kernel	3	3	3	3	3	3	1.5	1.5
B2 b.s. All cases	B2 bargaining set is empty.							
B* b.s. All cases	6	4	4	4	2	1	0	0
	Actualized pay-off is not in B* bargaining set, but is in B* bargaining set.							
Opp. Parties	J.S.P.	C.G.P.	J.C.P.	D.S.P.	S.D.F.			
Lower House	114	59	39	27	3			

N.L.C.: New Liberal Club J.S.P.: Japan Socialist Party
C.G.P.: Clean Government Party (Komei-to) J.C.P.: Japan Communist Party
D.S.P.: Democratic Socialist Party S.D.F.: Social Democratic Federation

Table 39 After the thirty-eighth general election, 1986

		Nakasone third cabinet, July 22nd				
	Tanaka	Nakasone	Suzuki	Fukuda	Komoto	Indep.
Lower House	87	62	60	56	28	13
Posts	Vice.Pr.	Prime	Finance	Educat.	Econ.Pl.	Gen.Mg.
Inside( )	(Just.)	Fore.gn	Home Af.	Agri.		
Assigned to	(Health)	Posts	Defence	Science		
Upper House	Trade Transp. Secret. Nat.land Enviro.	(Labor) Const.				
Pay-off	8	5	3	3	1	1
Big 3 of L.D.P.	Sec.Gen.		PARC	Ex.Coun.		
Proportional	5.97	4.25	4.12	3.84	1.92	0.89
Kernel	5.25	5.25	5.25	5.25	0	0
B2 b.s. Simple Maj; Incl. J.C.P.	6.5	4.5	4.5	3.5	1	1

Integer solution does not exist but for example

is in B2 bargaining set.

Table 39 continued

	J.S.P.	C.G.P.	J.C.P.	D.S.P.	N.L.C.	S.D.F.
B2 b.s. Simple Maj. Excl. J.C.P.	7	4	4	3	3	3
B2 b.s. Stable Maj. Incl. J.C.P.	7	4	4	4	1	1
	6	5	4	4	1	1
	6	4	4	4	2	1
	6	3	3	3	3	3
B2 b.s. Stable Maj. Excl. J.C.P.	6.5	4.5	4.5	3.5	1	
Opp. Parties Lower House	86	57	27	26	6	4

Integer solution does not exist but for example is in B2 bargaining set.

Table 40 After the thirty-ninth general election, 1990

	Takeshita (Tanaka)	Miyazawa (Suzuki)	Kaifu cabinet, February 28th Abe (Fukuda)	Watanabe (Nakasone)	Komoto	Indep.
Lower House	71	63	62	53	26	15
Posts	(Justice)	Health	Foreign	Trade	Prime	
Inside( )	Finance	Gen.Mg,	(Agri.)	Poss	Secret.	
Assigned to	Education	Defence	Transp.	Hokkaido	Enviro.	
Upper House	Const. Home Af. Nat.Land	Econ. Pl.	Labor	(Science)		
Pay-off	6	4	4	4	3	0
Big 3 of L.D.P.	Sec.Gen.	Ex.Coun.	PARC			
Proportional	5.14	4.56	4.49	3.84	1.88	1.09
Kernel	4.2	4.2	4.2	4.2	2.1	2.1
B2 b.s. All Cases	B2 bargaining set is empty.					

Table 40 continued

B* b.s. Actualized pay-off is not in B* bargaining set, but

	J.S.P.	C.G.P.	J.C.P.	D.S.P.	P&S	
Simple Maj. Incl. or	6	4	4	4	2	1
		or				
Excl. J.C.P.	6	5	4	3	2	1

is in B* bargaining set.

B* b.s. Actualized pay-off is not in B* bargaining set, but

	J.S.P.	C.G.P.	J.C.P.	D.S.P.	P&S	
Stable Maj. Incl. or	6	4	4	4	2	1
		or				
Excl. J.C.P.	6	5	4	3	2	1

is in B* bargaining set.

B* b.s. Actualized pay-off is in B* bargaining set and also

	J.S.P.	C.G.P.	J.C.P.	D.S.P.	P&S	
Stable Maj.	6	4	4	4	2	1
		or				
Excl. J.C.P.	6	5	4	3	2	1

is in B* bargaining set.

Opp. Parties	J.S.P.	C.G.P.	J.C.P.	D.S.P.	P&S
Lower House	141	46	16	14	5

P&S: Progressive Party and Social Democratic Federation

NOTES

1 Introduction

1 Under a presidential system like that in the United States, each candidate for congress is free to choose his or her ideological or political position to maximize his or her own chance of victory. But in a parliamentary system, since politicians in the same party form a cabinet together, it is difficult to have a different policy.

2 See Table 25.

3 Although no one has tried to explain L.D.P. factions in terms of cultural factors alone, Baerwald (1986, p. 17) dared to say, "to anticipate or wish that factionalism could or should be eliminated from the L.D.P., as its critics so ardently desire, is to expect this political party to become something other than a Japanese organization."

4 The L.D.P. was formed by the amalgamation of the Liberal Party and the Japan Democratic Party in 1955, but they had formed coalition governments before that.

5 The rule of the method of largest remainders is named the Hamilton method by Balinski and Young (1982).

6 See Table 25.

7 Sakagami (1966–80) introduced the story.

8 Kiyotaka Kuroda, the director of the Hokkaido Colonization Office, tried to sell the Office to his old colleague at a very low price.

9 The Upper House was formed mainly of peers who were the descendants of Daimyos (warlords), court nobles and the Hambatsu (feudal clique).

10 See Ito (1934) and Inada (1960, 1962) for the detailed story.

11 Voters were male, more than twenty-five years old and paying more than fifteen yen in direct national tax. This means that only 1.1 per cent of the population had the suffrage. But this may be understandable, if we remember that universal manhood suffrage was introduced in Italy only in 1912, Holland in 1917 and England in 1918. France, which introduced universal manhood suffrage in 1848, may have been the only large country to have universal male suffrage at a national level at the time. Since the number of voters is readily

95

available and exact, some researchers accepted it and said there was also unequal apportionment before World War II. This is not correct. Tables of population and apportionment appear in Appendix 2. (Tables 1 to 8)

12 The tax restriction became ten yen and the voters became 2.2 per cent of the population.

13 Constituencies were prefectures independent of cities that had more than 30,000 residents.

14 One of the reasons why government succeeded in carrying the amendment was the increase in the number of members of the Lower House. The figure went from 300 to 369 in 1900. After the amendments the seventh election in 1902, the first under this rule, was held with 376 seats. Tomita (1962–3) and Sakagami (1966–80) are the best references to consult.

15 S.N.T.V. was introduced to prefectural assemblies in 1899 and to city assemblies in 1911. Only the Upper House (the House of the Lords) continued to use multi-voting for mutual election. The House of Lords system itself was abolished after World War II and the multi-voting rule disappeared from Japanese electoral law.

16 It is interesting to note that Hara continued to use S.N.T.V. for sixty-eight two-member districts and eleven three-member districts which he created with 295 single-member districts. Tamai (1995a, b) mentions the possibility of gerrymandering. At the time the restriction of tax payment became three yen and 5.5 per cent of the population had the right to vote.

17 The Seiyu Kai won 282 of 464 seats.

18 Twenty per cent of the population had the right to vote.

19 The total number of House members went from 464 to 466. They divided some prefectures into districts in order that each district should have three to five members. Some scholars justified this on the grounds that the Goken Sampa tried to divide prefectures of the same size to match the prefectures with the smallest populations.

20 The Allies broke up the giant family-dominated financial and industrial combines known as *zaibatsu*, which had largely controlled the Japanese economy.

21 The Allies redistributed the land to tenant farmers and established independent yeomen farmers.

22 After apportioning 466 seats to the prefectures, they divided Hokkaido, Tokyo, Niigata, Aichi, Osaka, Hyogo and Fukuoka, which were apportioned fifteen seats or more, into two districts. The voters in one- to five-member districts wrote down one name, the voters in six- to ten-member districts wrote in two names and the voters in eleven- to fourteen-member districts wrote in three names.

23 The Upper House was formed mainly of peers who were the descendants of Daimyos (warlords), court nobles and the Hambatsu (feudal clique) until the new constitution took effect.

24 The Japan Liberal Party had 141 seats and the Japan Progressive Party had ninety-four seats. Both of them were conservative and became the basis of the L.D.P.

25 Thirty-nine female representatives at one time is still the record.

26 Under restricted multi-voting or single voting, even a minority like the communists can win a seat if the number of seats assigned to the district is five or more.

27 This ratio shows only an extremity and not the whole apportionment problem. Equalization of this ratio does not necessarily give a unique solution, and the American Lower House apportionment method (the "Hill method" as Balinski and Young 1982 call it) does not necessarily minimize the ratio. But since this ratio is most commonly used in Japan, I adopt it for illustrating the situations and call it "the ratio".

28 The Democratic Socialist Party, the Clean Government Party (Komei-to) and the Japan Communist Party are considered to be city parties.

29 Some Americans complain that the United States Supreme Court has become conservative because of the long rule of the Republicans. The Japanese case would be extreme.

30 To the best of my knowledge, Kobayashi (1989) is the only paper to appreciate this point.

31 See Curtis (1988).

32 See Hirose (1981) and Wada (1985).

33 *Minami-nippon-shinbun*, July 18th, 1985.

34 Kyogoku said, "it secures automatic redistribution." Inquiry of the Japan Election Studies Association (Hirano 1990) shows that his opinion is not an exceptional one. (See Table 27.)

2 A game theory analysis of Duverger's law

1 Sometimes southern Democrats and northern Democrats look to belong to different parties.

2 Famous examples are Canada and India. Canada's three-party system is usually explained by its strong geographical parties. India, where one big party and many small parties compete, is a disputable case. (See Riker 1976, 1982, 1986; Palfrey 1989; Humes 1990; etc.) Even England, which has a cabinet system, has a significant third party, though it is often cited as an example of a country with a two-party system.

3 In some case supporters of a third party vote for the party that stands second in their preference order.

4 Some of the supporters of a large party vote for the party that stands second.

5 Now they are forming a single party called Shinshin to (New Frontier Party).

6 In any case the J.C.P. would have candidates for all single-member districts. In the election game they may not be a good rational player.

7 This statement may look strange in the current situation where the L.D.P. and the J.S.P. organize a coalition government. A coalition in Tokyo just for the sake of retaining power creates serious chaos in the local electoral districts. Supporters in the local areas still understand the parties' characters like this.

8 We often see the situation of the chicken game in the real world. The original textbook story is as follows. A street gang plays a game on the road. Two boys drive cars down the center line from each direction. The one who runs straight is the winner and the one who exits from the line is called "chicken". The pay-off matrix would be

B\C	run	exit
run	(0,0)	(3,1)
exit	(1,3)	(2,2)

   The Nash equilibria are (exit, run) and (run, exit). But we cannot choose either one of them without a suitable focal point and any other outcome may happen, including "crash". The chicken game shows the difficulty of solving the multi-equilibria game.

9 To explain the Indian case where multi-party competition continues, Riker (1976) shows in his three-party model that, for three parties to survive, the center party must be the largest. (As Humes 1990, p. 230, says, Riker 1982, 1986 may have stated his proposition incorrectly.) Interestingly enough, our case 4 or 5 fits Riker's condition and result even though the mechanics are different.

10 An election with a run-off where the top two candidates can stand for the second election has a good chance of escaping from the possibility of the chicken game. If we change the second assumption of the setting to an election with a run-off, our two theorems would become as follows. *Negative theorem*: exit, which means implicit alliance, occurs only if the Condorcet winner is the smallest party. *Positive theorem*: the Condorcet winner always becomes the final winner.

11 See Riker (1986).

3 The Liberal Democratic Party as a coalition government

1 In 1983 the L.D.P. experienced coalition government with the New Liberal Club (N.L.C.), but the N.L.C. members had belonged to the L.D.P. before and almost all of them returned to the L.D.P. later. Actually the previous L.D.P. governor (party leader), Yohei Kohno, was the party leader of the N.L.C.

2 Sato and Matsuzaki (1986, pp. 6, 7), Inoguchi (1990), etc.

3 Leiserson (1967, 1968), Ishikawa (1978, p. 179; 1984, p. 217), Sato and Matsuzaki (1986, p. 32), Kanazashi (1989), Inoguchi (1990, 1991a, b), Kohno (1991, 1992), etc.

4 See Ishikawa (1978, p. 179; 1984, p. 217).

5 Table 26 shows how severe the competitions in S.N.T.V. are. In case A, Takehiko Endo would have borne a grudge against Michihiko Kano and Tetsuo Kondo. The competitions are tough in the J.S.P., too. In case B, Toshiharu Okada would have resented Ryuji Ikemoto. Over thirty such cases can be found in 129 districts.

6 Lijphart *et al.* (1986) among others uses the term "semi-proportional representation system" to introduce the S.N.T.V.

7 In cases where there was a strong faction leader who could wield strong procedural power there was no election.

8 Ishikawa (1978, p. 193; 1984, p. 244), Yoda (1985), Sato and Matsuzaki (1986, pp. 64, 65), etc.

9 Leiserson (1967, 1968) studied the minimum-winning coalition.

10 If cabinet seats are assigned in proportion to the parties' seats, the outcome should be (6.4, 4.6, 4.5, 1.2, 1.0).

11 See Appendix 1 for more information.

12 For the convenience of the reader, I summarize the notions and characteristics in our context in Appendix 1.

13 Under multi-member districts with an S.N.T.V. election system a new candidate cannot choose the faction to which his or her competitor, who is usually the incumbent, belongs, even if the ideology of the faction might be most suitable for him or her. The leader of the faction allows a powerful candidate to enter in order to make his faction larger, even if the ideology of the candidate is different. This makes for almost no ideological differences between the factions. Inoguchi (1989) analyzed L.D.P. politicians by questionnaire and found differences in policy tendencies between the factions, but the existence of such a study may itself show that there is almost no difference.

14 This fact is theoretically supported, too. See Cox (1994) for the theoretical proof. Taagepera and Shugart (1989) among others show the proportionality of seats and votes in Japan, but they also mention there is bonus for the large parties (the L.D.P. and J.S.P.). I am worried that they did not consider the fact that the L.D.P. and J.S.P. are based in rural areas where much *per capita* representation is apportioned.

4 The economic effect of the apportionment of representatives

1 Nordhaus (1975), Frey and Schneider (1979) etc.

2 Mayer (1984), etc.

3 Peltzman (1976), etc.

4 Olson (1965), etc.

5 Niskanen (1971) etc.

6 Mean voter result would be changed according to the allocation of physical capital.

7 For the Japanese case see Table 23.

8 We assume this to avoid the potential effects of the political process (e.g. redistribution) on capital and land. These issues have already been studied. (Mayer 1984, etc.) At least in Japan, since *per capita* savings are higher in agricultural areas than in city areas our conclusion will not be negated by this assumption. (We can consider that people in agricultural areas have both land and capital.)

9 We will assume these production functions are homogeneous of degree 1. Let us also assume

$$\frac{\partial^2 F}{\partial L_F^{\,2}} < 0$$

$$\frac{\partial^2 M}{\partial L_M^2} < 0$$

and for the sufficient condition of the interior solution

$$\lim_{L_F \to 0} \frac{\partial F}{\partial L_F} \to \infty$$

$$\lim_{L_M \to 0} \frac{\partial M}{\partial L_M} \to \infty$$

10 See Ishi and Koizumi (1981), Ishi *et al.* (1981, 1983). Fujimoto *et al.* (1983), Ogura (1984). I myself have done empirical work that includes consideration of redistribution (Wada 1985).

11 It may seem strange that all persons in a single representation member district will get the same benefit, since the single representative needs to guarantee the benefit to only 51 per cent of the population, but in a multiple representative constituency system like Japan's (choose three to five people per district without vote trading) this assumption may not be improper.

12 The Japanese expression "Cut the head off a living person" may illustrate the difficulty.

13 If you want to imagine the Japanese case, you might consider the time just after World War II as the first period, and the high growth era (the 1960s) and after as the second period.

14 We can get the same conclusion by starting with an increase in capital instead of a rise in international prices. We will not use this way, in order to avoid complicated equations, although it may be closer to the Japanese situation after World War II.

15 Because of the setting of the model, each individual's general income is the same. So for maximizing *per capita* general income we should maximize total general income or, excepting the benefits, "G.N.P." The G.N.P. without reapportionment will be

$$F(T, L_F - m) + \pi (1 + p) M (K, L_M + m)$$

The G.N.P. with reapportionment to get the proportionality will be

$$F(T, L_F - n) + \pi (1 + p) M (K, L_M + n)$$

The function

$$F(T, L_F - x) + \pi (1 + p) M (K, L_M + x)$$

will be maximized when

$$-\frac{\partial F(T, L_F - x)}{\partial L_F} + \pi (1 + p) \frac{\partial M(K, L_M + x)}{\partial L_M} = 0$$

or

$$\frac{\partial F(T, L_F - x)}{\partial L_F} = \pi (1 + p) \frac{\partial M(K, L_M + x)}{\partial L_M}$$

That is, x=n (see equation (40)).

16 When the price of the industrial goods rises, the people who were in the agricultural area in the first period will get $\hat{w}_F (1 + c)$ if they stay in the agricultural area or $\hat{w}_M$ if they move to the industrial area. Since each production function is

$$\{\hat{l}_F\}^a \, T^{1-a}$$
$$\{\hat{L}_M\}^b \, K^{1-b}$$

Before labor moves, each wage will be (let L_F and L_M be the first period equilibrium):

$$a\{(1 + c)L_F\}^{a-1} \, T^{1-a} \, (1 + c)$$

and

$$\pi(1 + p)b \, \{(1 + c)L_M\}^{b-1} \, K^{1-b}$$

So they will not move until

$$a\{(1 + c)L_F\}^{a-1} \, T^{1-a} \, (1 + c) < \pi(1 + p)b \, \{(1 + c)L_M\}^{b-1} \, K^{1-b}$$

that is,

$$(1 + c)^{1+a-b} < (1 + p)$$

(The income from land and capital does not depend on place of residence and before the population movement the benefits are also the same. We do not need to consider them at this stage.)

17 From (47)

$$\pi(1 + p) = \frac{\dfrac{\partial F(T, (1 + c) (L_F - n))}{\partial L_F} (1 + c)}{\dfrac{\partial M(K, L_M(1 + c) + n)}{\partial L_M}}$$

From (46)

$$ms = \frac{(L_F - m) (L_M + m)}{L}$$

$$[\pi(i + p) \, \frac{\partial M(K, L_M(1 + c) + m)}{\partial L_M} - \frac{\partial F(T, (1 + c) (L_F - m))}{\partial L_F} (1 + c)]$$

101

d = (47) L.H.S. − (46) L.H.S.

$$d = (1 + c) \left[\frac{\partial F(T, (1 + c)(L_F - n))}{\partial L_F} - \frac{\partial F(T, (1 + c)(L_F - m))}{\partial L_F} \right]$$

$$+ \frac{T}{L} \left[\frac{\partial F(T, (1 + c)(L_F - n))}{\partial T} - \frac{\partial F(T, (1 + c)(L_F - m))}{\partial T} \right]$$

$$+ \pi(1 + p) \frac{K}{L} \left[\frac{\partial M(K, L_M(1 + c) + n)}{\partial K} - \frac{\partial M(K, L_M(1 + c) + m)}{\partial K} \right]$$

$$- \frac{ms}{L_F - m}$$

Substitute $\pi(1 + p)$ and ms, and if we consider d as a function of m, D(m), D(n)=0 and D'(k)<0(m<k<n). Therefore:

D(m)>0   d>0

(F and M are homogeneous of degree 1.)

BIBLIOGRAPHY

Aichi Kengikaishi Hensan Iinkai (1953). *Aichi Kengikaishi* (Aichi Kengikai, Nagoya).

Alesina, R., and N. Roubini (1990). Political Cycles in OECD Economies. *NBER Working Paper* No. 3478.

Araki, Y. (1992). Sengo Dai 1 kai no Sosenkyo to G.H.Q. *Mimeograph*.

Asano, D. (1990). Senkyo Seido no Hensen, in Yomiuri Shinbunsha Chosa Kenkyu Honbu (ed.) *Nihon no Senkyo, Sekai no Senkyo* (Yomiuri Shinbunsha, Tokyo).

Asano, K. (1988). Senzen Senkyo niokeru Choson Tani no Shudan Tohyo, *Senkyo Kenkyu* Vol. 3.

Austen-Smith, D. (1987). Parties, Districts and the Spatial Theory, *Social Choice and Welfare* Vol. 4.

Baerwald, H. (1986). *Party Politics in Japan* (Allen & Unwin, Boston).

Balinski, M., and H. P. Young (1982). *Fair Representation* (Yale University Press, New Haven).

Brams, S., and P. Straffin (1982). The Entry Problem in a Political Race, in P. Ordeshook and K. Shepsle (eds.) *Political Equilibrium* (Kluwer–Nijhoff, Boston).

Cox, G. W. (1991). S.N.T.V. and d'Hondt are "Equivalent", *Electoral Studies* Vol. 10.

—— (1994). Strategic Voting Equilibria under the Single Non-Transferable Vote, *American Political Science Review* Vol. 88.

—— and E. Niou (1994). Seat Bonuses under the Single Non-Transferable Vote System, *Comparative Politics* Vol. 26.

—— and F. Rosenbluth (1993). The Electoral Fortunes of Legislative Factions in Japan, *American Political Science Review* Vol. 87.

—— and F. Rosenbluth (1994). Reducing Nomination Errors: Factional Competition and Party Strategy in Japan, *Electoral Studies* Vol. 13.

Curtis, G. L. (1988). *The Japanese Way of Politics* (Columbia University Press, New York).

Duverger, M. (1951). *Les Partis Politiques* (Armand Colin, Paris. English Translation by B. and R. North, 1954).

—— (1986). Duverger's Law: Forty Years Later, in B. Grofman and A. Lijphart (1986).

103

BIBLIOGRAPHY

Egami, T. (1981). Gikai no Kino, in Y. Iizaka and F. Horie (eds.). *Gikai Demokurasi* (Gakuyosha, Tokyo).

Feddersen, T., I. Sened and S. Wright (1990). Rational Voting and Candidate Entry under Plurality Rule, *American Journal of Political Science* Vol. 34.

Frey, B. S., and F. Schneider (1979). An econometric model with an endogenous government sector, *Public Choice* Vol. 34.

Fujii, T., and Y. Ishikawa (1993). Hyogoken niokeru Dai Ikkai Sosenkyo, *Senkyo Kenkyu* Vol. 8.

Fujimoto, S., Y. Oiwa, H. Kawanobe, K. Kurokawa and A. Yokoyama (1983). Yosanhaibun to Seijiyoso, *Kokyo Sentaku no Kenkyu* Vol. 3.

Fukunaga, F. (1986). Sengo niokeru Chusenkyokusei no Keisei Katei, *Kobe Hogaku Zasshi* Vol. 36.

Fukushima, M., and R. Tokuda (1939). Meiji Shonen no Chosonkai, *Kokka Gakkai Shi* Vol. 53.

Fukuzawa, Y. *Fukuo Jiden* (Iwanami Bunko, Tokyo).

Greenberg, J., and K. Shepsle (1987). The Effect of Electoral Rewards in Multiparty Competition with Entry, *American Political Science Review* Vol. 81.

Grofman, B., and A. Lijphart (eds.) (1986). *Electoral Laws and Political Consequences*. (Agathon Press, New York).

Gunma Kengikai Jimukyoku (1951). *Gunma Kengikai Shi*.

Haruhara, G. (1962a). Mura Yakunin no Senkyo, *Jichi Kenkyu* Vol. 38.

—— (1962b). Machi Yakunin no Senkyo, *Jichi Kenkyu* Vol. 38.

—— (1963). Mura Yakunin no Senkyo to Shunin, *Jichi Kenkyu* Vol. 39.

Hirano, H. (1990). Senkyoseido ni kansuru Yuushikisha Chosa, in Nihon Senkyo Gakkai (ed.) *Senkyoseido Kaikaku no Shoso*. (Senkyo Kenkyu Series No. 4.) (Hokujusha, Tokyo).

Hirose, M. (1981). *Hojokin to Seikento* (Asahi Shinbunsha, Tokyo).

Horie, F. (1992). Sengo Dai 1 kai Sosenkyo so Deta teki Rekishi teki Bunseki. *Mimeograph*.

Humes, B. (1990). Multi-party competition with exit: a comment on Duverger's Law, *Public Choice* Vol. 64.

Ide Family (1629–1874). *Documents*.

Imai, S. (1989). Daitoshi Shikai Giin 3 Kyu Renki Senkyo no Hikaku Kenkyu, *Yokohama Shiritsu Daigaku Ronso* Vol. 40.

Inada, S. (1960, 1962). *Meiji Kenpo Seiritsu Shi* (Yuhikaku, Tokyo).

Inoguchi, T. (1983). *Gendai Nihon Seijikeizai no Kozu* (Toyo Keizai Shinposha, Tokyo).

—— (1989). Seisaku Kettei heno Ishikikozo wo Miru, *Ekonomisuto* Vol. 67.

—— (1990). The Emergence of a Predominant Faction in the Liberal Democratic Party: Domestic Changes in Japan and their Security Implications. *Mimeograph*.

—— (1991a). Gendai Nihonseiji no Seikaku to Kino, *Shiso* No. 805.

—— (1991b). Jiminto Kenkyu no Hukugoteki Shiten, *Leviathan*. Vol. 9.

Ishi, H., and I. Koizumi (1981). Daitoshi ni Cyuzetsu Nihonzaisei no Bunpai Kozo, *Shukan Toyo Keizai*, Kindai Keizaigaku Series Vol. 56.

Ishi, H., T. Hasegawa and K. Hata (1981). Jueki to Hutan no Chiiki Kozo Bunseki, *Kikan Gendai Keizai* Vol. 46.

BIBLIOGRAPHY

Ishi, H., T. Hasegawa, K. Hata and M. Yamashita (1983). Jueki to Hutan no Chiikibetsu Kichaku to Hojokin no Yakuwari, *Keizaikikakucho Keizaikenkyujo Kenkyu Series* Vol. 39.

Ishikawa, M. (1978). *Sengo Seiji Kozoshi* (Nihon Hyoronsha, Tokyo).

—— (1981). *Nihon no Seiji no Ima* (Gendai no Rironsha, Tokyo).

—— (1983). Doken Kokka Nippon, *Sekai* No. 453.

—— (1984). *Deeta Sengo Sejishi* (Iwanami Shoten, Tokyo).

—— (1985). *Nihonseiji no Toshizu* (Gendai no Rironsha, Tokyo).

—— (1990). *Senkyoseido* (Iwanami Shoten, Tokyo).

Ito, H. (1934). *Kenpo Shiryo* (Kenpo Shiryo Kanko Kai).

Ito, T. (1989). Endogeneous Election Timings and Political Business Cycles in Japan. *NBER Working Paper* No. 3128.

Iwai, T. (1988). *Rippo Katei* (Tokyo Daigaku Shuppankai, Tokyo).

—— (1991). *Seiji Shikin no Kenkyu* (Nihon Keizai Shinbunsha, Tokyo).

Jichi Daigakko (1960). *Sengo Jichishi* III (Okurasho Insatsukyoku).

—— (1961). *Sengo Jichishi* IV (Okurasho Insatsukyoku).

Jichisho. *Shugiin Senkyo no Jisseki 1-20 Kai, 21-39 Kai.*

Jichisho Senkyobu Senkyoka (1985–87). Senkyo Seido no Hensen 1-13, *Senkyo Jiho.*

Kanagawa Kengikai Jimukyoku (1953). *Kanagawa Kenkaishi.*

Kanazashi, M. (1989). Habatsu – Jiminto wo Ugokasumono, in Y. Sone (ed.) *Nihon no Seiji* (Nihon Keizai Shinbunsha, Tokyo).

Kawahito, S. (1992). *Nihon no Seito Seiji 1890–1938* (Tokyo Daigaku Shuppankai, Tokyo).

Kishimoto, K. (1985). Chusenkyokusei no Keisei to Futsu Senkyoho, *Reference* Vol. 35.

Kishimoto, K. (1986). Kizokuin Soshiki to Kaiha no Hensen, *Reference* Vol. 36.

Kobayashi, Y. (1989). Nihongata Chuusenkyokusei no Tokushitu, in S. Watanabe (ed.) *Senkyo to Gisekihaibun no Seido* (Seibundo, Tokyo).

Kodaira, O. (1985). Nihon no Fudo to Senkyo, *Jurist* Vol. 38.

Kohno, M. (1991). Jiminto – Soshiki Riron karano Kento, *Leviathan* Vol. 9.

—— (1992). Rational Foundations for the Organization of the Liberal Democratic Party in Japan, *World Politics* Vol. 44.

Kokumin Sansei 95 Shunen, Fusen 60 Shunen, Fujin Sansei 40 Shunen Kinenkai (1985). *Senkyo ni Rekishi ari.*

Komei Senkyo Renmei. *Shugiin Senkyo no Jisseki 1-30 Kai.*

Kawamura, M. (1942). Meiji Jidai niokeru Senkyoho no Riron oyobi Seido no Hattatsu, *Kokka Gakkai Shi* Vol. 56.

Laver, M., and N. Schofield (1991). *Multiparty Government.* (Oxford University Press, Oxford).

Leiserson, M. (1967). Jiminto toha Renritsu Seiken to Mitsuketari, *Chuokoron* No. 959.

—— (1968). Factions and Coalitions in One-party Japan: an Interpretation Based on the Theory of Games, *American Political Science Review* Vol. 62.

Lijphart, A., R. L. Pintor and Y. Sone (1986). The Limited Vote and the Single Non-Transferable Vote: Lessons from the Japanese and Spanish Examples, in B. Grofman and A. Lijphart (eds.) *Electoral Laws and their Political Consequences* (Agathon Press, New York).

BIBLIOGRAPHY

McLure, C. (1983). Fiscal Federalism and the Taxation of Economic Rents in G. Break (ed.) *State and Local Finance: the Pressures of the 1980s* (University of Wisconsin Press, Madison).

Matsuo, T. (1989). *Futsu Senkyo Seido Seiritsushi no Kenkyu* (Iwanami Shoten, Tokyo).

Mayer, W. (1984). Endogenous Tariff Formation, *American Economic Review* Vol. 74.

Mieszkowski, P. (1983). Energy Policy, Taxation of Natural Resources, and Fiscal Federalism, in C. McLure (ed.) *Tax Assignment in Federal Countries* (Centre for Research on Federal Fiscal Relations, Australian National University, Canberra).

—— and E. Toder (1983). Taxation of Energy Resources, in C. McLure and P. Mieszkowski (eds.) *Fiscal Federalism and the Taxation of Natural Resources* (Lexington Books, Lexington).

Mitake, N. (1992). Dai 25 Kai Teikoku Gikai Shugiin Hireidaihyo Hoan no Seiritsu, *Senkyo Kenkyu* Vol. 7.

Mueller, D. C. (1989). *Public Choice* II. (Cambridge University Press, Cambridge).

Myerson, R., and R. Weber (1993). A Theory of Voting Equilibria, *American Political Science Review* Vol. 87.

Nakamura, A. (1987). Seito to Habatsu, in Y. Iizaka, N. Tomita and N. Okazawa (eds.) *Seito to Demokurashii* (Gakuyo Shobo, Tokyo).

Nishizawa, Y. and M. Kohno (1990). Nihon niokeru Senkyo Keizai Junkan, *Leviathan* Vol. 5.

Niskanen, W. A., Jr. (1971). *Bureaucracy and Representative Government* (Aldine, Chicago).

Nordhaus, W. D. (1975). The Political Business Cycle, *Review of Economic Studies* Vol. 42.

Ogura, M. (1984). Doro Jigyohi no Chiikikan Haibun no Koritsusei, *Kikan Gendai Keizai* Vol. 58.

Olson, M. (1965). *The Logic of Collective Action* (Harvard University Press, Cambridge, Mass.).

Ordeshook, P. (1986). *Game Theory and Political Theory* (Cambridge University Press, Cambridge).

Owen, G. (1982). *Game Theory*, second edition (Academic Press, Orlando).

Ozawa, I. (1993). *Nihon Kaizo Keikaku* (Kodansha, Tokyo).

Palfrey, T. (1984). Spatial Equilibrium with Entry, *Review of Economic Studies* Vol. 51.

—— (1989). A Mathematical Proof of Duverger's Law, in P. Ordeshook (ed.) *Models of Strategic Choice in Politics* (University of Michigan Press, Ann Arbor).

Peltzman, S. (1976). Toward a More General Theory of Regulation, *Journal of Law and Economics* Vol. 19.

Ramseyer, J. M., and F. M. Rosenbluth (1993). *Japanese Political Market Place* (Harvard University Press, Cambridge, Mass.).

Reed, S. (1991). Jiyuminshuto no Koteika, *Leviathan* Vol. 9.

Reed., S. (1994). Thinking about the Heiritsu-sei: a Structual-Learning Approach, *Kokyo Sentaku no Kenkyu* Vol. 24.

BIBLIOGRAPHY

Riker, W. (1976). The Number of Political Parties, *Comparative Politics* Vol. 9.

—— (1982). The Two-party System and Duverger's Law: an Essay on the History of Political Science, *American Political Science Review* Vol. 76.

—— (1986). Duverger's law Revisited, in B. Grofman and A. Lijphart (1986).

Sakagami, N. (1966–80). Senkyo Seido Ron Shiko, *Senkyo* Vols. 19–33.

—— (1989). Wagakuni niokeru Senkyoseido to Giin Senshutsu Mondai no Shiteki Kosatsu, *Tokyo Toritsu Daigaku Hogakkai Zasshi* Vol. 30.

—— (1990). *Gendai Senkyo Seidoron* (Seji Koho Center, Tokyo).

—— (1991). A History of the Japanese Electoral System, *Bulletin of Tokyo Gakugei University, Sect. III* Vol. 42.

Sakai, M. (1989). Senzenki 2 dai Seito Tairitsu kano Senkyo niokeru Chiho Shidosha no Jidaishugiteki Keiko, *Senkyo Kenkyu* Vol. 4.

Sartori, G. (1976). *Parties and Party Systems* (Cambridge University Press, Cambridge).

—— (1986). The Influence of Electoral Systems: Faulty Laws or Faulty Method? in B. Grofman and A. Lijphart (1986).

Sato, S. (1991). Meiji Chuki niokeru Fukenkai Kisoku to Shugiin Senkyoho no Keisei, *Shakaikagaku Kenkyu* Vol. 11.

—— (1992). 1900 nen Taisei no Seiritsu to Dai 7 kai Sosenkyogo no sono Koka. *Mimeograph.*

—— and T. Matsuzaki (1986). *Jiminto Seiken* (Chuo Koron Sha, Tokyo).

Sawa, T. (1990). Meiji Saishoki no Senkyo Seidoron no Hatten, *Senkyo Kenkyu* Vol. 5.

Schofield, N. (1978). Generalised Bargaining Sets for Cooperative Games, *International Journal of Game Theory* Vol. 7.

—— (1982). Bargaining Set Theory and Stability in Coalition Governments, *Mathematical Social Sciences* Vol. 3.

—— (1987). Bargaining in Weighted Majority Voting Games, in M Holler (ed.) *The Logic of Multiparty Systems* (Kluwer, Dordrecht).

—— and M. Laver (1985). Bargaining Theory and Portfolio Pay-offs in European Coalition Governments 1945–83, *British Journal of Political Science* Vol. 15.

Schofield, N., and M. Laver (1987). Bargaining Theory and Cabinet Stability in European Coalition Governments 1945–83, in M. J. Holler (ed.) *The Logic of Multiparty System* (Kluwer, Dordrecht).

Shepsle, K. (1991). *Models of Multiparty Electoral Competition* (Harwood, Chur).

—— and R. Cohen (1990). Multiparty Competition, Entry, and Entry Deterrence in Spatial Models of Election, in J. Enelow and M. Hinich (eds.) *Advances in the Spatial Theory of Voting* (Cambridge University Press, Cambridge).

Shubik, M. (1981). Game Theory Models and Methods in Political Economy, in K. J. Arrow and M. D. Intriligator (eds.). *Handbook of Mathematical Economics* Vol. 1, (North-Holland, Amsterdam).

—— (1982). *Game Theory in the Social Sciences.* (MIT Press, Cambridge, Mass.).

Shugiin Sangiin. *Gikaiseido 70 Nenshi Shiryo* (Okurasho Insatsukyoku).

BIBLIOGRAPHY

Snyder, J. M. (1989). Political Geography and Interest Group Power, *Social Choice and Welfare* Vol. 6.

—— (1990). Election Goals and the Allocation of Campaign Resource, *Econometrica* Vol. 57.

Soma, M. (1986). *Nihon Senkyo Seido Shi* (Kyushu Daigaku Shuppan Kai).

Suetake, Y. (1993). Meijikoki Taishoki Daisenkyokusei to Seiji Shakai. *Mimeograph.*

Taagepera, R., and M. S. Shugart (1989). *Seats and Votes* (Yale University Press, New Haven).

Takemae, E. (1986). Sengo Shoki no Senkyoseido Kaikaku, *Tokyo Keidai Gakkai Shi* Vol. 148.

Tamai, K. (1995a). Hara Takashi Naikakukano Shosenkyokusei Seiritsu Katei, *Hogaku Kenkyu* Vol. 68.

—— (1995b). Hara Naikakukano Shosenkyokusei Donyu nitsuite. *Mimeograph.*

Thayer, N. B. (1969). *How the Conservatives Rule Japan* (Princeton University Press, Princeton).

Tominomori, E. (1992). *Nihongata Minshushugi no Kozu* (Asahi Shinbunsha, Tokyo).

Tomita, N. (1960a). Jiyu Minken Ronja no Fusen Shiso, *Seikei Ronso* Vol. 29.

—— (1960b). Nihon Fusen Undo Shi Josetsu, *Seikei Ronso* Vol. 29.

—— (1960, 1962, 1963). Dai 14 Teikoku Gikai niokeru Senkyoho Kaisei, *Seikei Ronso* Vols. 29, 31 and 32.

—— (1986, 1987). Shugiin Sosenkyo no Shiteki Bunseki, *Senkyo Kenyu* Vols. 1 and 2.

—— (1990). Fusenho no Seitei to Dai 1 kai Sosenkyo, *Senkyo Kenkyu* Vol. 5.

Toyama, S., and Y. Adachi (1961). *Kindai Nihonshi Hikkei* (Iwanami Shoten).

Tuchida, E. (1991). Chiho Gikai Seido Shoshi, *Reference* Vol. 41.

Wada, J. (1985). Seijikatei no Keizaigakuteki Bunseki Nihon niokeru Politico-Economics Model no Tekiyo, *Hermes* Vol. 36.

—— (1988). Giin haibun no keizaiteki eikyo, *Hitotsubashi Ronso* Vol. 100.

—— (1990). Bargaining Theory and Portfolio Pay-offs in Japanese Government. *Mimeograph.*

—— (1991). Giseki Haibun no Hoho toshiteno Saint and Lague Hoshiki, *Kokyo Sentaku no Kenkyu* Vol. 18.

—— (1992). A Game Theoretical Study of "Duverger's Law", *Yokohama Shiritsu Daigaku Ronso* Vol. 43.

—— (1993a). Jiminto Seiken keisei no Gemuronteki Bunseki, *Kokyo Sentaku no Kenkyu* Vol. 21.

—— (1993b). Liberal Democratic Party as a Coalition Government, Yokohama City University Discussion Paper Series No. 52.

—— (1994a). A History of Japanese Election Rule. Yokohama City University Discussion Paper Series No. 62.

—— (1994b). Heiritsusei no Kenkyu: Kozo Gakushu ron karano Bunseki niyosete, *Kokyo Sentaku no Kenkyu* Vol. 24.

—— (1995a). Japanese Election System: Three Analytical Perspectives. Ph.D. dissertation (University of Maryland).

BIBLIOGRAPHY

—— (1995b). Shosenkyoku Hireidaihyo Heiritsusei ni kansuru Gemuronteki Ichikosatsu, *Senkyo Kenkyu* Vol. 10.

Weber, S. (forthcoming). On Hierarchical Spatial Competition, *Review of Economic Studies*.

Weber, S. (1990). On the Existence of a Fixed-number Equilibrium in a Multiparty Electoral System, *Mathematical Social Sciences* Vol. 20.

Yamamuro, T. (1993). Showa Shoki niokeru Senkyoku Seido to Seijishakai. *Mimeograph*.

Yoda, H. (1985). Jiminto Habatu to Naikaku Keisei, *Kokyo Sentaku no Kenkyu* Vol. 6.

INDEX

110